SAVE HARMLESS AGREEMENT

Because use of the information, instructions and materials discussed and shown in this book, document, electronic publication or other form of media is beyond our control, the purchaser or user agrees, without reservation to save Knowledge Publications Corporation, its agents, distributors, resellers, consultants, promoters, advisers or employees harmless from any and all claims, demands, actions, debts, liabilities, judgments, costs and attorney's fees arising out of, claimed on account of, or in any manner predicated upon loss of or damage to property, and injuries to or the death of any and all persons whatsoever, occurring in connection with or in any way incidental to or arising out of the purchase, sale, viewing, transfer of information and/or use of any and all property or information or in any manner caused or contributed to by the purchaser or the user or the viewer, their agents, servants, pets or employees, while in, upon, or about the sale or viewing or transfer of knowledge or use site on which the property is sold, offered for sale, or where the property or materials are used or viewed, discussed, communicated, or while going to or departing from such areas.

Laboratory work, scientific experiment, working with hydrogen, high temperatures, combustion gases as well as general chemistry with acids, bases and reactions and/or pressure vessels can be EXTREMELY DANGEROUS to use and possess or to be in the general vicinity of. To experiment with such methods and materials should be done ONLY by qualified and knowledgeable persons well versed and equipped to fabricate, handle, use and or store such materials. Inexperienced persons should first enlist the help of an experienced chemist, scientist or engineer before any activity thereof with such chemicals, methods and knowledge discussed in this media and other material distributed by KnowledgePublications Corporation or its agents. Be sure you know the laws, regulations and codes, local, county, state and federal, regarding the experimentation, construction and or use and storage of any equipment and or chemicals BEFORE you start. Safety must be practiced at all times. Users accept full responsibility and any and all liabilities associated in any way with the purchase and or use and viewing and communications of knowledge, information, methods and materials in this media.

www.KnowledgePublications.com

For my Father, Mel Larsen, Edwin York and Cresson Kearny

Copyright, 2006

By

www.KnowledgePublications.com

Contents

Title	Page

Dedication and Preface ii

Why Waste is Good iii

This Book, Solar energy, and the Future of Energy iv

Free Solar Panels 1

Free Glass and Mirrors 4

What to Do With All That Glass 7

A Twenty-five cent Window Heater 9

Making a Solar Oven for $9 12

Uses for a Solar Oven 17

Solar Hot Water Heater 19

Desalination 21

Excellent Websites 22

The Solar Puddle 23

Free Fresnel Lenses 25

Free Insulation 27

Ice Making and Air Conditioning 28

Heat Exchangers for Hot Water and Cooling 31

Steam Distillation 34

New House Construction 36

Updates To This Book and Energy Philosophy. 38

Civil Defense & Solar Ovens. 39

About the Author 41

www.KnowledgePublications.com

Dedication & Preface: To Judy A. Harris.

This book is dedicated to my mother, Judy A. Harris, who has shown me since childhood that one person's waste is another person's treasure. All through my childhood, we would take what others would discard and give it to those in need: 100-pound bags of beans from farmers in Michigan, crates of slightly overripe fruit from the produce store, three-day-old cookies from the bakery, and much more. We would pick up these items and personally deliver them to people such as the single mother who was just barely making ends meet, and the 80-year old lady who could not afford fresh fruit on her social security, *to people who had less than nothing, and to people who were only missing a little something.* Mom would take the cookies and horse-trade them to other people for physical items that were not going to be thrown away. Free cookies were used as barter to get needed items.

There are tens of thousands of donated baby quilts and comforters covering infants and children around the world who are sick, in the hospital, or terminally ill because Mom would get material (cloth) donated, found or contributed. We would drop it off to old ladies and other people who had nothing to do, and in many cases, were house bound. These people relished the opportunity to again have a duty and a method of contribution. Mom and the ladies still do this independently, as well get together every Tuesday (without fail) to have a large quilting bee with twenty or thirty people, and many times more. Material that would have been waste is keeping people warm around the world. People who were alone now have community, and minds that would atrophy now have something to occupy thoughts and something to look forward to every day. This is what free material can do; sometimes, it is more valuable than gold. There is a secret to getting free material for your efforts. This book will share some of these methods with you.

This book is NOT about dumpster diving or trash-picking. Our best practices are much simpler, easier and cleaner. All you have to do is ask. If you are afraid to ask someone to save something for you when they are going to throw it out, then return this book right now for a refund.

You would be amazed what happens when you ask. What's the worse they'll say? Just a simple no.

When you ask, the world opens up.

Companies who install new windows have to haul the old windows back to the shop, after which the glass is thrown in the dumpster. The glass company has to pay for the dumpster to be emptied. By giving you the old glass, they actually save on dumpster fees.

It is in our nature as humans to help. Most people will happily save items for you if they will be used for something. Most people get a lot of joy from giving. Even if what they are giving away is deemed useless to them, they know you see it as a treasure.

There are high school teachers who have read this book and are now getting free glass for solar ovens for teaching physics. There are Boy Scout troops making solar ovens for almost nothing, and there are people doing experiments and learning in this exciting field of energy because they can now obtain the necessary items for experimentation and learning.

The world opens up when you ask. Thanks, Mom.

www.KnowledgePublications.com

Why Waste is Good

There is no advancement without waste. There must be the ability to test something and break it. The ability to make mistakes in development work is where discovery is made and improvements are forged. Without the capability of having a surplus of material so multiple versions can be developed, compared, and analyzed side by side, there IS no advancement. For example, if a person has ONE of something, they are not going to do experiments with it and risk it being lost. If sand were as scarce as gold, transistors would have never been invented, let alone developed to the state that they are today.

This philosophy is good for modern development work and engineering, such as designing vehicles, computers, and even the silicon in the chips that are found in everything that is around us today. It also applies to the home experimenter in you. Why haven't you done solar experimenting on a large scale, for perhaps your entire house? The answer is probably because of the cost of glass. "What size do I get? Do I need two pieces? When it expands from the heat, will it break? I really want a big oven, but that requires $200 in glass alone, etc." We are always finding reasons NOT to do something. This book is going to show you how to get enough glass and other free items to build a solar oven, NOT one that is one foot by one foot, but FOUR FEET by EIGHT FEET.

There will be more than enough glass to waste, break, drop, or to make mistakes with. In doing my research for the writing of this book, I lost about one in every ten pieces of glass for various reasons. The glass was broken either in hauling, moving, experimentation, or by the neighbor kid (Anthony and his slingshot). Once, I accidentally left a double piece of glass lying on a black metal surface in the sunshine. Well, the sun heated the black metal, which heated and expanded the first layer of glass that was in contact with the hot metal. That piece of glass expanded at a different rate than the second layer of glass and...well, when I came back from Home Depot, I had a shattered pieces of glass on my hands. Oh well, I have twelve more pieces just like it, and I just learned something :)

Some of the biggest businesses were started from someone else's waste product. Back in the early 1900's, "gas" for cooking and lighting was made in a steam reformation process of coal. This made carbon monoxide and hydrogen gas (for more on this, get the Hydrogen & Fuel Cell Video at **www.Knowledge- Pub-lications.com**). The process was not ran at the high temperatures that are used today. It also formed byproducts, most of which was a sticky, stinky, black mess called COAL TAR. This was something the gas companies had to pay to have hauled away. This coal tar was a treasure trove of chemicals, one of those being just what was needed for the manufacture of red dyes. At that time in history, a red dye was hard to make and very expensive. Well, a small company started using the coal tar to make dyes, other pigments, and then a whole family of chemicals, resulting in the company's growth. Maybe you've heard of the company, The BASF Corporation.

I could fill this book with examples of businesses that were started from another companies' waste, but this book is about using waste to gain knowledge through experimentation as well as to make solar energy related items, many of which can be sold, and all of which are fun.

Remember, waste is good. Next time you see waste, look at it as an opportunity to make something else, an opportunity to make money, and an opportunity to learn (and have fun).

[iii]

This Book, Solar Energy and the Future of Energy

What is the future of energy, and what is it going to look like? Where should a person study and learn to be a player in the energy future rather than a participant.

People ask me these questions all of the time. I have been deep into the energy business for many years doing experiments, development work, and very focused on the subject of energy. I understand the role of energy in human life. I know the history of energy and invention I also understand the human spirit, and the instinct to drive forward and improve. I understand energy from 8000 years ago to 500 years into the future. I've worked on many confidential research projects regarding energy, and what could have been done 100 years ago, 40 years ago and what we can do today. And not only what we can do today with our engineering and manufacturing, but what we can do tomorrow and a few years from now. If you knew what I know right now, you'd be staying awake all night like an excited child who just saw Star Wars for the first time. The possibilities are endless. I'll be sharing a little secret with you in this book.

This book is very low tech. It is a hands on, how-to-do-it-in-your-backyard, book. For those who want to be a part of the excitement of the future energy business, this book is a better primer and instructional tool than any fancy $100 books. They discuss long formulas and contain discussion about fuel cells and new generation photovoltaic and other items on the front page of Popular Mechanics.

The real future of energy is not Proton Exchange Membranes (PEM) powering vehicles and homes, or Solid Oxide Fuel Cells (SOFC), and it sure as heck is not solar cells on roof shingles (what a failure). The strength we have in year 2003 is not the new technology. It is our ability to do mass manufacturing with world-class economics. In our wonderful disposable society (which is good), we make things faster and cheaper and in greater varieties with newer versions quicker and easier than we ever have before. It is only through mass manufacturing and 21st century material science that we will make solar energy so affordable that it is actually disposable. Imagine a disposable solar energy device.

The future of energy is not in hard-to-make membranes for expensive fuel cells and one billion dollar solar cell manufacturing facilities. Here's the little secret...the future of energy is made of iron, steel, aluminum, copper, plastic and glass. We know how to mass manufacture these items cheaper and faster than at anytime in history.

This certainly does not sound as sexy as the stuff that Popular Mechanics uses to put on their front page. All they care about is selling magazines, and most of their writers are English and Journalism majors. The articles are dumbed down to the lost, common reader.

What is the future of energy? It looks like many of the items in this book uses wood, metal, glass and plastic, and the sunshine that is falling on your head all day long. This book contains the fundamentals that you must understand to be a future player in the energy field.

The items in this book are mass manufactured in such quantities that most of the items get thrown away. A smart person can get glass, wire, wood, metal, and more, for free. A 20-year old glass door will work as well as a new piece of glass for a solar heater. All you have to do is hose it off and maybe clean the inside.

These are the fundamentals and YOU can LEARN them YOURSELF in your yard. This does NOT require going to college or buying expensive books or expensive equipment. If a person wants to be in the energy field, it is incumbent upon that person to teach himself or herself.

This is 100 to 200-year old technology that we can use to make energy today with 20th and 21st century materials.

My objective with this book is a hope that the reader can start learning and experimenting with energy TODAY instead of just reading Popular Science magazine and dreaming about working with energy.

FREE SOLAR PANELS

These panels cost me absolutely nothing, that is, free. I just hauled them away. How? Where? This is one of the reasons you bought this book, right? Have you seen flashing "arrow" signs on the highway near road construction? Many of these are solar powered. The alpha numeric signs that flash words and numbers are also solar powered. These bulbs used in the sign to make the flashing arrows used to be powered by diesel engines, such as the Lister diesel engine. Now these signs are powered by solar panels, large batteries, and LED based illumination. A simple "arrow board" trailer typically has two 55-watt Siemans panels on it with two or three "8D-sized" lead acid batteries. Each battery weighs about 200 pounds. Imagine this heavy trailer with six hundred pounds of batteries, several hundred pounds of metal, being hit by a drunk driver (BOOM). Well...it happens all the time. Drivers hit these things on a VERY regular basis, especially during the wintertime. The panels end up getting "cracked." Actually, the glass laminate on top of the polycrystalline solar cells gets cracked while the cells themselves are typically okay. Thousands of cracks will run around on the surface of one panel making the top of the solar panel "less clear." Thus, the glass absorbs some of the incoming solar light, which gets turned to heat rather than striking the solar cells. These panels, that were 55 watts when new, now put out 15 to 25+ watts for me in the Michigan summer sunshine. But, they were free. When NEW (2001), each 55-watt panel costs $230-$330. My cost for the fractured panel at half-output was $0. In October of 2002, I had over sixty panels like this. That's free energy. As you drive down the highway and see these arrow boards, take note of the names of the company on the arrow board. These are generally NOT owned by the state, and those are generally NOT state workers out there. The workers you see are a contracted construction company and they RENT the arrow boards from a rental company. Approach the rental company and ask them to save the broken solar panels for you. They normally throw these in the trash. The insurance company for the construction company will pay the rental company for the damaged panels.

A friend of mine and I put ten panels on a frame made of 2x4's, and we wired the panels up. Three men and myself manhandled this up a ladder and onto my roof. We should have only put five panels on a frame rather than ten, as it was a little heavy. Nevertheless, after a few screws, a bunch of wire, and some wood, I had free electricity on top of the house. The panels feed into a battery bank in the basement, which is connected to a simple 1750-watt modified sine wave inverter. I do the charge controlling manually. With these, I power the lights and the fans in my basement. I do this typically during the daytime when I am

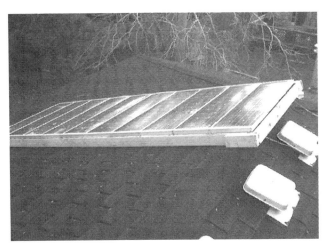

down there working. Sometimes when it is hot, I just hook up the solar panels to the 12-volt blower in my homemade "air conditioning" system. If I add a good trace inverter/charge controller to the system, wire it into my house box, and put up some more of the solar panels, I'll have a nice system. I still have about forty more panels to put up. The wiring and the frame take time. Half my house is shaded from 1PM to 7PM by a big tree, but that keeps the house cooler in the summer. As you read this book, you will find that most of my solar work is in areas OTHER than photovoltaic (PV). The only reason I have these up is because the panels were free, plus I like to have panels up catching sun that I can use for charging batteries used in other experiments I am doing.

I've frequently said that I think photovoltaic solar panels are the WORST thing that ever happened to the solar energy field. It seems people thought this was the "nirvana" and the "pinnacle" of solar energy that could be reached, but no one bothered to do the math. PV panels take ten to fifteen years to pay back their money. Also, consider the amount of electricity it took make the silicon. Regardless of the faulty articles some solar power magazines have put out, a 6th grader can calculate the Return-On-Investment numbers. There are more inexpensive ways of making electricity with solar energy, and there are ways that are far more efficient. The inexpensive ways are typically less efficient, but are made of nothing but iron, steel, copper, aluminum and other mass manufactured components such as pipes and tubing and glass or plastic. The solar-based systems that are very efficient typically involve extremely high temperatures beyond the abilities of metals. For an in-depth discussion of this subject, see my other book, *The Positive Promotion of Hydrogen Energy, A Model for Success in an Economically Driven Market*. When it is available, it will be at **KnowldgePublications.com**.

Sunshine to Dollars is NOT going to be the typical solar energy book you read. This book is going to SHOW YOU HOW to do experiments around YOUR house with simple tools and inexpensive or FREE materials. This book will ENABLE you, not just tell you about things you can only dream about or that are out of your reach. It is the authors' opinion that the largest value from this book is the FREE GLASS that can be easily obtained. Even free solar panels won't lower your electricity bill. There is still a charge associated with getting an inverter and with the life cycle of storage batteries. Making a solar heater and blowing hot air in even ONE room directly reduces fall/winter/spring-heating bills. Batteries for solar electric systems must be replaced approximately every five years, and cost hundreds to thousands of dollars. Glass, wood, and insulation in a solar air heater can last for twenty to fifty years and cost only a few dollars. Every major solar project in the world has failed due to poor economics and principle. Don't let your home experiment fail for the same economic reasons.

These are the highway construction "arrow boards" I am referring to. This one is folded over for transport, and the solar panels that normally point straight up can be seen. These are two 55-watt Seimens panels. These panels are okay and working fine. I'm waiting for a drunk driver to hit this so I can get them for free.

This is my pickup truck loaded with about 25 solar panels. Some of the panels are bent, and all of the panels have a cracked laminate on top of the solar cells. All of the panels DO work and will output energy in the sunshine. One of the alpha numeric highway signs can be seen in the background. These larger signs have six 80-watt Seimens panels and about twelve Trojan six-volt "golf cart" batteries. I've not seen a drunk driver hit one of these yet. If one does, he'll get what he deserves, and I'll get a bunch of free solar panels and maybe some free batteries. The guys who run the sign rental company will be getting some hot corn bread and beer when I show up to get the panels. It is always good to show our appreciation to the people who are saving the panels for you. Something fresh and delicious goes a long ways and is always appreciated.

FREE GLASS
(the best value in this book!)

FREE glass can make solar ovens, solar water heaters, solar hot air heaters, and anything you want solar. All this glass is double insulated (two sheets), tempered safety glass, and it is all free. If I can get all I want, so can you. I looked in the yellow pages and called some glass and window companies. Several were ALL TOO HAPPY for me to come pick up the glass. This saves them from paying for the dumpster that the glass goes into. Since I work for a non-profit organization, I even offer to give them a receipt for tax donation purposes. Many of them don't even want to bother with that, but are glad to get rid of their glass. They set the glass aside for me and I come by at least once a week and pick it up. If someone is going to save glass for you, make sure you stop by and keep it out of their way. When they call and say, "Come get the glass," you get over there fast and get it. I prefer to get the glass that was removed from sliding glass doors. These are typically 34" x 76" and have two sheets of "safety glass." Safety glass is hard to break unless you hit a sheet on the edge. When these do break, the sheets break into 'rock salt'-like bits, in size and shape, that are easily swept up. They don't break into large shards that will act like a guillotine and cut your hand, arm, leg, face or body. The glass in the photo (bottom right) in wood frames is also double insulated glass. This makes it easier for me to include these in experiments because I have wood I can screw into, making the pieces more manageable. The free glass I get is not "perfect." Many times, the glass is slightly fogged due to moisture getting in between the glass sheets because of a seal failure. That doesn't bother us in a solar heating system. The solar heat will quickly drive off any water in the glass, and a little silicone will plug any holes after the water is driven out. Right now, I have enough free glass to cover my entire roof if I so desired. Further chapters in this book will show the glass being used for passive solar heating and for a solar oven.

FREE MIRROR

I got all the free mirror I needed from one glass supplier. The mirror was to be used for brand new condos and the sheets had a few very, very faint scratches in the surface. This was unacceptable for a $300,000 condo, but as a reflection surface for a passive heater, this is great. I got 1/4" plate mirror, but all kinds can be found for free. I would suggest using a thinner glass mirror, as the 1/4" stuff is heavy, and is NOT safety glass. You can easily get cut if it breaks. I got over 200 square feet of mirror for free from one glass supplier.

Wear SAFETY GLASSES and USE GLOVES. Don't be afraid to ask the glass guys EXACTLY

These doors will be turned into outstanding solar ovens for baking bread and cooking other items. The glass will be at a forty-five degree angle to the sun, reflectors will be off the top and the bottom, and the walls will be made up of the free foam core doors and foam core door knockouts pictured in this book.

These glass doors can also be used in a "flat" box type solar oven as documented further in this book. Again, the wood around the glass makes it very easy to attach a reflector on hinges or the wood of an insulated solar oven.

Other framed, double pane, insulated window glass is seen on the bottom left of this photo. The doors are double-sheet, tempered safety glass. These doors would cost over $200 each. The glass is over $100 if bought new (if not more). These six doors were FREE and will make great solar heaters or ovens.

I got all this glass in one day. It took less than thirty minutes to drive to the glass shop, load the glass, drive home, and unload it. This is not the same glass pictured on preceding pages. This is additional glass, and there was much more on the way at the time I was writing this book. I currently have enough glass to cover my entire roof with solar heating. This glass is being used to make the greenhouse enclosure for the front porch documented in this book.

"...and its available for free…if you go at night."

This is the punch line to the old joke, but this is no joke. I got everything you see loaded on the back of my pickup truck all for free, just for the asking (not going at night). I got all this in one day and it took less than thirty minutes of effort. Included in the haul of treasures are two 1800-psi CO_2 tanks. I can use these for storing natural gas, hydrogen, air, or any other gaseous products. The next most inexpensive brand new tanks would be SCUBA diving tanks that are about the same size but can be rated up to 3000 or 3600 psi.

The satellite dishes came from a company that installs DIRECT TV. Ask your local Circuit City and Radio Shack what company installs the dishes they sell. Approach that company and ask for junk dishes. I got the CO2 tanks from someone who moved into a new building and discovered the old tanks in there. They threw the tanks out.

I have six "broken" solar panels that will output half their energy. This was from the road sign rental company that rents signs to road construction crews (see previous chapters). I have six 18" satellite dishes with the metal dish and the supports for the LNB and the roof mounts. The dishes will be coated with a reflective surface (aluminum foil works) and used for solar concentration. The mounts make it easy to mount the dish, a solar panel, a passive solar heater, or solar oven on a wall or a flat surface. This makes it easy to point the solar collector up and down or side-to-side directing it towards the sun. I have three large pieces of insulated safety glass for solar ovens or solar heaters, and I have about five smaller pieces of the same type of glass. This glass was removed from houses when a local glass company installed new glass. The wood frame around the glass actually makes it easy to attach and mount the window to whatever solar experiment or invention I am working with. The glass had a thin film tint on it, but a sharp knife and a can of $1 carburetor cleaner took the film and its adhesive off the glass in just a few minutes.

WHAT TO DO WITH ALL THAT GLASS

This is a marked up photograph of the front and side of my simple little house. I have inserted lines to show where I am going to build a 'greenhouse' type of appendage onto the house. I will start by enclosing in about three fourths of the front porch with glass. For this I am going to use the sliding glass door glass I got for free. I'll make a simple custom frame for the front porch with two by fours and one by twos to hold in the glass. The system will be modular and bolt together such that I can take it down with about 30 minutes worth of work in the late spring. I am NOT doing this as a permanent addition for several reasons. I don't want to have to go get permits and such and this is an EXPERIMENT. I will have temperature probes and data recording devices monitoring the weather, the sun shine and the temperature in the 'green house'. This will allow me to make improvements and additions to the front greenhouse. The concrete porch will server as a crude heat sink and I'll use a blower to move air from the house into the greenhouse on the porch, the hot air will then enter the front window and move into the house. I have lines drawn on the front of the house (the part that is not the porch) and I could put a simple green house there, however I don't think I'll make something that large. I might make two or three solar hot air heaters from two or thee sheets of glass, but these will be below the windows and above the bushes.

The shingles on the southern part of the roof need replacement soon. Right now half the bad area is covered with PV panels I got for free and the other half will be covered with glass as part of a solar hot air heater. I think glass will make a better roofing material than the shingles. Also, the tempered sliding glass door glass can take one heck of an impact so it should be VERY resistant to hail. We have taken a hammer and beat the middle of the tempered glass sheets. It took 6 hard hits before the glass shattered. ONLY TEMPERED glass will behave this way. Regular glass will break with a very small impact, be careful!

A solar oven and air heater will go into the window where the air conditioner is just above and to the right of my pickup truck.

[7]

If you live in a glass house, don't throw rocks. I am glassing in part of the front porch, making it a small greenhouse. With the double wall insulated glass, it got warm quickly allowing hot air to enter the house. I was unable to complete this the way I wanted to because the city wanted a permit for the construction. The permit price was based on the cost of the construction, which was $18 for new 2x4's. The inspector could not believe I got all of the glass for free and how low the whole thing cost. I decided this was more of a headache than I needed at the moment in my neighborhood, so I elected to take down the glass porch. It took less than 30 minutes with a power screwdriver. Less than an hour later, it was as if it were never there. As I mentioned before, it was modular and intended to be put up and taken down with ease and not as a permanent addition to the house.

I ended up making a simple hot air heater for the front southern window. The photos show the heater without the insulation on the in and out air ducts. The air ducts are the aluminum tubes used for cloths dryer venting. The glass is free. The back of the heater is 1/2" plywood painted black, and there is a piece of two-inch foam behind it attached with liquid nails. A frame of 2x4's keeps the glass off the black wood, and a 2x4 runs down the center from the top to about twelve inches from the bottom. The air enters at the top, is blown down the air heater, and comes back up the other side (because of the 2x4 divider in the middle), and then exits the top as it goes into the house. This very crude setup would blow 105°F air into the house anytime the sun was shining. There are two reflectors on each side to add more sunshine to the heater. There is a thermostat from Grandier in the middle of the heater. When the air is 100°F, it turns on a six inch $20 heating duct blower from Home Depot that moves the hot air into the house. I forgot to plug in the blower one day and the heater quickly got over 200°F and melted the plastic on the thermostat <sigh>. There are better ways of making a solar heater but this is a great start and learning exercise.

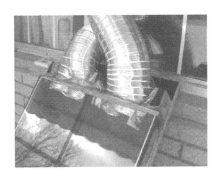

A Twenty-five Cent Window Solar Energy Heater That Works

www.KnowledgePublications.com www.SunshinetoDollars.com
Steven Harris h2fuel@mail.com

Black plastic taped to a curtain rod over a window

Vertical blinds UP

Sides of plastic are open. Its just a hanging sheet of black plastic

Air gap between the bottom of the plastic and the window sill, only one to two inches

77°F air OUT of the top with February sunshine in Michigan

3-Mil black plastic from Home Depot, costing a few dollars per roll

67°F Room Air IN the bottom air gap

Inside View

Outside View

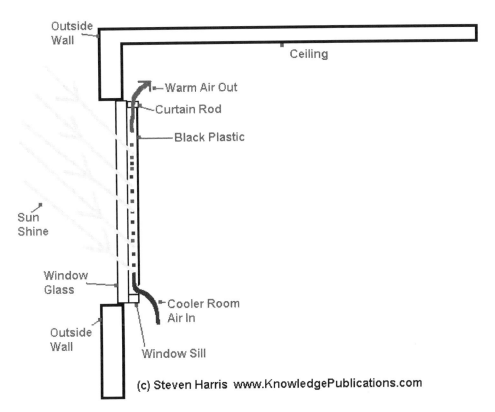

WHY IS THIS DIFFERENT?

What is different about this and sunshine just falling into a room? In Thermal Science, it is called QUALITY. Simply put, heat quality is the temperature of the energy. When sunshine normally falls into a room, it will hit the carpet, a desk, a paper, a wall, or a sleeping dog. All of these items reflect, absorb, and bounce the light in a different fashion. Some light gets bounced onto the ceiling where part of the energy gets absorbed and reradiated as heat, while some of it gets reflected to other parts of the room. The black plastic sheet is VERY receptive in the absorption of sunlight, and absorbs most of the sunlight in one limited spot of air between the plastic and the glass. This reduces how fast the heat can get away and allows the air to get hotter (have a higher quality). The black plastic absorbs the ultraviolet (visible and infrared wavelengths of sunlight) that make it through the glass, and re-radiates the energy as long wavelength infrared light. You can mildly feel this on your face when standing close to the plastic. Cool air thermally siphons from the bottom of the plastic, warms up, and moves out the top of the plastic/window air gap. This simple trick noticeably warms the room up, making it feel much more pleasant. The whole window can be blocked with plastic, or only part of it can be blocked to save some of the view.

I used a three Mil, black piece of plastic I got from Home Depot, but a black trash bag will work almost as well.

MORE SUNSHINE = MORE HEAT
With a Word of *Caution*

I added a reflector outside the window to bounce more sunshine into the window. This actually puts "TWO Suns" onto the window, the sun that normally falls through the window and the reflected sunlight. This is called TWO SUNS. If I had a second reflector, this would be a total of "Three Suns" (DO NOT DO THIS). Before the sunshine hid behind the clouds last four days here in Michigan, this reflector quickly got my air out temperatures above 85°F, and the sunshine was a little hazy. With my solar oven experience, I think this would of easily gotten over 100°F with a February sunshine in Michigan. The reflector is aluminum foil with Elmer's glue on cardboard. I am going to re-do this with flat masonite. Adding a hinge or two allows for easier adjustments (rather than using the displayed brick method.) DO NOT add more than ONE reflector to your unit. When it gets warmer and the sun gets stronger, multiple reflectors *WILL* actually get the plastic so hot that it WILL literally go POOF and up in flames. ONE reflector with REGULAR aluminum foil is more than enough.

It is true that in areas like Michigan, we have a limited number of sunny days in December. However, we have more sunny days in January, February and March, but it can EASILY be well below freezing during these months. Even during April and May, it can be in the forties, fifty's and sixties. I LIKE my house 70°F+, and on these days during half the year, this little solar air heater will add gentle warmth that my furnace or wood stove does not have to add. It does it all by itself. I don't have to turn it on. The project can be done in ten minutes, and I can take it down and put it up in seconds. This project can also be done by anyone in an apartment.

Making a 350°F+, Twenty Loaf of Bread, Solar Oven for $9

This is the FREE 34x76 inch piece of sliding glass door glass coming home from the Glass and Mirror company. It is slightly fogged but will work great.

Glass and metal liner for size comparison. It will work.

This is the metal liner inside an upright freezer. I took the outside walls, mechanical refrigeration and other components off for experiments and was left with just the metal liner.

Finish painting it black. It took four cans at $1 each to paint the whole INSIDE flat black. You do not need to paint the outside. It took about 45 minutes to do the job, and could have been done as well with a brush and black paint from a can.

Paint it black with a $1 can of flat black spray paint from Home Depot.

I put the metal liner on top of the door from the old freezer for insulation. I actually added MORE pink home insulation between the liner and the old freezer door (not shown), as it needed more insulation. Styrofoam from Home Depot/Lowe's is inexpensive and will work. Using a few inches of free cardboard will also work. A variant of a layer of cardboard and a layer of Styrofoam will work. Straw bales and shredded newspaper will also work. The pink insulation I used was free because the bag was ripped and the store could not sell it.

Wanting to see how well the unit might work, I wrapped it in pink insulation and propped it up with some wood and chairs to keep it from falling over. I then started doing temperature measurements to see how hot it would get. Verifying the project as it goes along like this is called good development work.

FREE CARDBOARD, free walls, free insulation. The local appliance store was happy to give me a box of boxes. I couldn't take just one or two...I had to take a whole load. They normally sell things for recycling, but were happy to give a load to me for my experiments. All of the insulation you see in this project can be replaced with cardboard and air spaces. I'd use three or four layers of cardboard with one or more inches of air gaps between the layers to replace the eight inches of double-wrapped pink insulation I used. Solar ovens can be as small as one cubic foot. They don't have to be this big. The free cardboard can be used for making any size solar cooker or solar heater. Just waterproof it with glue and plastic.

Next, I made a one-piece, three-sided wall from the cardboard, covered with a reflective layer. This can be normal aluminum foil or it can be mirror sheeting. The mirror sheeting will give a little better result. I paid eleven cents a square foot for mine from http://www.mirrorsheeting.com. I used 3M spray adhesive to glue the sheeting to the cardboard. Elmer's glue will also work but does not dry as fast. Spread the glue on, brush it out with a brush, and then lay on the aluminum foil or sheeting material. I could use my free, one-quarter inch plate glass mirror, but it would have been a little heavier and harder to handle.

I also put a wrapping of cardboard around the insulation to keep it from falling.

Nielsen Enterprises:
Hydroponic Gardening/Reflective Films, Mirror Sheeting.
3019 S 256th Street, Kent, WA. 98032
(253) 941-7425
9AM to 9PM (Pacific Standard Time)

The FIRST TEST CAKE (top left). Cake from a box mix ready to go into the oven, and a type K thermocouple meter reading a temperature of 295°F. Get a four-dollar oven thermometer from the hardware or grocery store.

Right Photo: The finished cake, forty-five minutes later. The cake normally bakes at 325°F. During the first part of the baking, the temperature fell to 240°F but came back up. The cake took only a few minutes longer to cook. Solar ovens can take more time to cook than a conventional oven. The positive side is that it is almost impossible to burn something in a solar oven. You hardly have to worry about over cooking.

After the first test cake, I baked five loaves of bread and two cakes at the same time. This time, the baking temperature was about 275°F because I added a lot of dough, which contains moisture. Driving off the moisture during the baking process will lower the temperature. However, it only took an hour and a half in Michigan June sunshine to bake these. All were baked at the same time. I estimate I could bake twenty loaves at once in the solar oven, and I could do four or five such batches during one solar day. That means this oven could bake eighty to one hundred loaves of bread in one full sunshine day. I imagine that if I cook two layers of loaves, I could bake almost twice as much. The baking time might extend just a bit and bring my over all numbers down from less than a doubling. Still, a hundred loaves a day, and $10 for the oven is not a bad investment. Start a Solar Bakery.

Complete photo documentation can be found at http://www.StevenHarris.net/solaroven.html
(~34 high resolution photos)

A Solar Oven with FREE GLASS, and Plywood and Foam from Home Depot.
The Wood, Foam, Screws, Adhesive and Metal Brackets cost about $15 in 2002.

We started with a piece of free glass with a wood frame around it. The frame was 24x24 inches, so we cut out a box with half inch plywood. The base of the plywood box is 24x24 inches, and the sides are 24x12 inches high. The oven will be twelve inches deep. At the same time, we cut two inches of foam to match the same sizes as the pieces of wood. This is the insulation. A wood box was made by screwing the sides and bottom together using metal corner brackets for 2x4's used in construction (about fifty cents each at Home Depot). We used sixteen metal corners.

Using a caulk gun and liquid nail adhesive, we glued the foam to the outside of the wood box. The foam sticks very quickly and only needs to be held in place for a few seconds. The foam is the outside of the solar oven. We did not add an additional protective layer. If the oven was going to be moved and transported, I might suggest gluing a layer of one-quarter inch plywood or some other laminate to the outside of the foam as an impact barrier and a layer of protection. Using our oven dimensions, we could build two complete ovens from one sheet of plywood and foam. However, because of this sizing, we could not make the foam larger to make a perfectly covered corner. But since there is so little exposed surface area in the corner of the oven, this will not represent a significant heat loss. Making a solar oven is NOT rocket science, and it is hard to goof. A solar oven is nothing more than a black box with insulation, two layers of glass on the top, and shiny reflectors. That's it. Just make sure to silicon all of the cracks and holes. A solar oven or heater will NOT work very well if there are air leaks.

Aluminum foil on the reflector.

The wood framed glass was attached to the plywood part of the box with a pair of $2 hinges from the hardware store. This enables the top to hinge backwards, but it is not necessary. The solar oven will work just fine if the glass is placed on the top and simply removed when desired.

The reflector operates differently from the oven. The wood for the reflector is not attached or hinged to the solar oven. The reflector just sits on the top of the solar oven and either the entire oven is rotated to track the sunshine, or the reflector is rotated by itself. This needs to be done every thirty to sixty minutes with a solar oven of this style.

The reflector IS hinged, so the shape of it can be changed. The idea is to concentrate the sunshine into the oven from two or three different locations. This increases the concentration of the sunshine and the maximum temperature of the oven.

To stick the aluminum foil or Mylar film to the reflectors, a glue was made from two parts Elmer's glue and one part water. Pure glue or 3M spray adhesive can also be used. When the glue is dry, the solar oven is ready for use. Don't forget to paint the inside of the oven flat black. A $1 can of flat black spray paint will work just fine. Both are available at Home Depot or Lowes.

For a simple and quick cooking experiment, get a can of biscuits or a load of frozen bread dough from the grocery store. To cook the biscuits, just unwrap them, put on a cooking sheet, and stick it in the solar oven. Remove the biscuits when they reach a nice golden brown color.

Too cook the frozen bread dough, let the frozen dough thaw and rise in a bread loaf pan. Then simply put the bread and pan into the oven and watch it bake. This could take twenty minutes to a few hours, depending on your sunshine. I usually bake a loaf in about an hour. Don't fear if the bread is left for too long in the oven. Solar ovens generally will NOT burn what is being baked. Bread is usually baked at about 350°F and biscuits are baked at about 425°F. Even if the oven is at 250°F, both of these will bake just fine.

To make soups and such, just put a dark pot (with no plastic handles) into the oven and put the ingredients in. This will heat up and cook pretty quickly. It is easier to bake soups than it is bread.

Yes, you can even bake a turkey in here if you so desire. Anything that will bake in a regular oven can be baked in a solar oven. Bread, biscuits and cakes are my personal favorites.

USES FOR A SOLAR OVEN.
I have to admit that I think cooking with a solar oven is just plain neat. There is something magical about putting bread out in the sunshine and coming back an hour later and it is all done. No electronics, no controls, and no on or off button...it just works. It is like a magic box, but it is not magic. It is plain and simple science.

TIME SAVER
There are some solar ovens that are built into the side of a house, either on the east or west sides facing south or in a southern wall (in the northern hemisphere of course). But most of us will use a solar oven sitting outside on a table or on the ground. The solar oven can be a time saver because of its "non-automation automation." Since it is very hard to burn anything in a solar oven, it is hard to cook something for too long. If you leave biscuits in the gas or electric oven in your house for three minutes too long, the biscuits get burned. If you leave biscuits for thirty minutes too long in a solar oven, they are just kept warm. It is easy to make up a pot of stew and some pans of cake or bread and simply put all of the items in a solar oven at once. Then, you can go about your business or errands for a few hours and come home to a fully cooked meal (assuming it did not get cloudy).

THIRD WORLD
This is where most of us Americans would say, "Boy, that'd be good in the third world." Well, I've done a lot of work with people in the third world, and they'd be happy just to have something to eat rather than something to cook it in. Most places that need the solar oven the most don't have the resources available to make an oven. Glass can be quite expensive, and often time is just not available. Glass can be heavy and obscure in size, and this makes it hard for people such as missionaries to transport it to a far away place. COOKIT is a great solar oven made out of nothing but cardboard, aluminum foil and a high temperature oven bag. You can see it at http://www.solarcooking.org/cookit.htm.

CIVIL DEFENSE in America.
As I sit here writing this updated page for the revised *Sunshine to Dollars*, Homeland Security Director Tom Ridge is telling us about home preparedness and the ready.gov website. I've worked in the civil defense field for nineteen years, and have helped and taught many people and families about home preparedness. There is NO substitute for preparedness...none. A little bit goes such a long way when things go bad.

WHAT KILLS PEOPLE, WHY ARE WE ALIVE TODAY?
Why is our world blessed with over six billion living souls today and growing? This is an easy answer...antibiotics and clean water.

Antibiotics are part of the modern medicine that keeps us alive. Imagine dieing of a small scratch from a rose bush or the bacterial infection after a viral infection such as a cold. Presidents Washington, Harrison, and Garfield all died of one type of infection or another. Antibiotics and modern medicine, the tools of research and production, all run on energy. Dow Chemical would not be producing much salicylic acid (aspirin) without energy.

Fresh water. It takes a significant amount of energy to move water. Whether it is up from a depth of one hundred feet down in Lake Huron, or one thousand feet down in the desert, or from twenty feet down the earth, it requires energy for pumping. Without fresh water that has been filtered through the soil, we are forced to drink surface water. Surface water with access to sunlight and oxygen is a good place for the growth of bacteria, viruses (in bacterial), parasites and other forms of contamination from fecal matter and other organic waste materials.

Energy for fresh water also implies energy to pump sewage OUT of a high-density population area. A modern city could not exist if there was not energy to pipe water INTO the city and energy to move the human excrement (piss and crap) OUT of the city. We also need energy to pick up our garbage and haul it out. All of these waste products are breeding grounds for bacteria and disease that has plagued and killed man.

What kills most of the people in a large hurricane, a flood, a nuclear detonation is the loss of infrastructure after the event. No power, no lights, no refrigeration, no heating, no water, no sewage, no banks, no ATM's, no delivery trucks, no gasoline, no natural gas, no telephones, no Internet, no cell phones...all this and more kill.

How Does A Solar Oven Help My Family in a Disaster?
It supplies a little bit of the energy that kept you alive but is now gone.

Thirsty? Did you get some water from a lake and don't know if there are little buggies floating in there that will cause stomach problems or an infection? Put the water in the solar oven and get the water to 160°F+ for at least six minutes. This will pasteurize the water and kill all but the most hearty of microbes (like what "might" be growing in a swamp). Boiling the water (at 212°F) in a solar oven for five to ten minutes will kill everything. You can install a distillation column (see elsewhere in the book) by attaching it to the solar oven (like what's on top of a moonshine still), and you can distill off the water vapor, condense it, and the water will be about as pure as fresh rain. You could even distill your own urine. Put a bucket of urine in a solar oven, boil the liquid, distill off the water, and drinkable water is produced. The only thing left will be heavy salt water. Fresh urine is sterile, with no bacteria. The nitrates and minerals in our urine are food for bacterial growth. A bacteriam that gets in there from the air or the container grows at a rapid rate. What happens to a pail of day old, stinky urine (the stink is from bacterial growth) in a solar oven? Well, it will heat up to about 212°F, killing all of the bacteria. The water then boils off, is condensed, and used. I should note that this method is also a very excellent method of doing desalination (removing salt) from seawater. Human urine is little more than salt water with minerals. Do you think whales don't piss in the ocean?

Hungry? Baking is a very energy intensive activity, usually because of the amount of time involved. Dutch ovens use a large amount of wood for baking. A "camping" oven on a burner takes a large amount of energy. Boiling water for soup can take five minutes, while baking bread takes thirty to sixty minutes. Every minute a burner is running amounts to one less minute worth of fuel you have to run a stove.

Corn bread (add water only mix), biscuits, cake and other baked goods are very inexpensive and very easy to bake, but only with electricity for lights and power for the oven. Without a modern oven, baking uses a lot of precious fuel and energy. Mixing up a batch of (add water only) biscuits using a Coleman oven stove can easily use a half pint to a pint of fuel, that is, if you have the $28 oven, $35 stove, and Coleman fuel at $3 per gallon, or gasoline at $1.50 to $2.00 a gallon and $1 gallon container to hold the fuel.

Fast, Cheap Emergency Food.
Take a small box of corn bread mix, add water, mix it up, pour it in a cake or bread pan and put it in a solar oven. When it is golden brown, remove it, let cool, and eat. For biscuits, just add water, roll out about one quarter to one third inch thick, cut it with an upturned cup, place the biscuits in the solar oven, and bake until golden brown. Add peanut butter, jelly, honey or anything else desired.

BISCUITS FROM SCRATCH?
Two cups flour
Less than one cup of water
One half to one teaspoon salt
One tablespoon baking powder
Zero to one half cup sugar

This is really hard tack (which is not hard when fresh). The easy way to remember this recipe is two, one, and one half. That is, two cups flour, one cup water, and a half teaspoon salt. The baking powder makes it puff up (like a biscuit), and the sugar adds calories and is optional. Mix this up, roll it out on a flat surface with a soda or wine bottle, cut it with the top of a cup, and put the biscuits in a solar oven (or regular oven). Eat fresh or let the biscuits dry out. They will keep for years. I have 2+ year old biscuits that are 100% edible. What spoils in food is the oils, butter, and milk products. However, adding oil, milk, powdered milk, or butter to the above recipe GREATLY improves the taste, but you need to eat them within a week of baking the biscuits. Breads with yeast, quick breads, unleavened breads, biscuits, drying meeting, dehydrating fruits, cooking beans, rice and many more items can be cooked with a solar oven. A complete class in preparedness is beyond the scope of this book but we felt that the subject was so important, and that solar ovens are so beneficial that we added this subject into the book.

Lack of energy kills people. Energy is life. Restricting, legislating regulating, or removing energy whether by government, man, or nature, kills humans.

A Solar Hot Water Heater Made from a Door, 2x4's, Plastic Sheeting, and Glass.

This is very easy. Take one door and put a 2x4 inch frame around the edge ON TOP of the door. Lay down a layer of plastic and pour in fifteen to thirty gallons of water. Cover it with a layer of double-sheet glass, like the glass from a thirty by seventy-two inch sliding glass door.

Make sure the 2x4 frame is the same size as the glass. The door under it can be bigger. In the photos above, I painted the door black and used clear plastic so the frame and construction method would be easy to see. However, I suggest NOT painting the door and just using black plastic sheeting. This is four-Mil, black plastic sheeting from Home Depot. There is about $2 in plastic used in this heater. The corners of the 2x4 inch frame are just screwed together with two three-inch, deck style wood screws. That's it.

WARNING. This water is HOT and WILL SCALD AND BURN YOU INSTANTLY. SEVERE BURNS ARE POSSIBLE *157.6F Shown on Meter*

Simply lay the sliding glass door over the frame. It seals nicely with the plastic. As the photo on the right shows, this water got to 157°F. I routinely get my hot water heaters to 185°F in the summertime, and easily get to 140°F to 155°F in the wintertime. This is done with NO REFLECTORS. If reflectors are added similar to the ones on the solar oven, the water will EASILY reach 212°F and boil away. This can be a good thing. Using a reflector is also a great way to catch more low angle winter sunshine to make more hot water. Heating a house with hot water is not as efficient as hot air. It takes about three times as many solar water collectors to heat a house than it does with solar hot air. BUT, in many cases, water is easier to work with and move. When your materials are FREE or cheap, the hot water method can be affordable. Don't try this with NEW materials. You will never get your money back.

These two top photos show some improvements on the hot water heater. I used the free door knockouts as additional insulation under the door. The photos clearly show the wood frame and how it was made to fit the glass going on top of it rather than the door under it. Notice the door on the right is NOT black, but white. It does NOT need to be painted if black plastic is used. The right photo shows the two solar water heaters that ran in my backyard for almost a year. Everyday, the water would get to about 180°F in the summer and around 150°F to 160°F in the winter, except when it was cloudy. I put about fifteen gallons of water in each one of these, but each one could hold thirty gallons. To have each one hold more water, just use 2x6 or 2x8 inch material for the wood frame instead of the 2x4's I used. Modify, experiment, and write me. Send photos!

Heating water up to 160°F for eight minutes or longer will kill most of the bacteria, spores and parasites in water. Please see the article in this book on the "Solar Puddle," and the section on Civil Defense. Not only can this make hot water, but it can also make water that is safe to drink. This is important for third world applications as well as disaster situations in the USA. Parasites and contaminated water kill more people around the world than anything else. Clean water, septic systems, antibiotics, and plentiful energy are the reasons we have over six billion people on the planet today. Eliminate any one of these items and people die.

DESALINATION - Salt Water to Fresh Water

Build it...I dare you. The solar hot water heater on the previous page is about as simple as it gets. Call some glass companies in the phone book and ask for some 34x72 inch "door wall glass" they have removed from a house when they installed a new sliding glass door. Go to the Habitat for Humanity store and get a door for $1. Find one on the curb, buy a used one, or ask the glass company if they have any old doors they removed. Get three 2x4's from Home Depot for about $2 each, and make the solar hot water heater I described. If you do this, and put fifteen gallons of water or more in it, it will be obvious to the person who actually does this experiment that even though the water might only be at 180°F, a great deal of water vapor (steam) escapes when the door is lifted a bit. It just shoots right out. It almost burns your hands sometimes (wear a pair of gloves when lifting the glass). To everyone else who just reads this book and does none of the experiments, the rapid steam generation will not be apparent.

ONE SUN. On a good and hot summer day with full sunshine in Michigan, the water will get to be about 180°F. It is hard to get much higher with just the sun falling on the glass. When the sun is falling on an object, this is called ONE SUN. When the sun falls on an object and a reflector (like a mirror or something shiny), the reflector reflects the sun onto the same object. This is called TWO SUNS. With two suns on the water, the energy input is almost doubled, and the water will BOIL. Yes, it will boil with stream bubbles and everything. This will produce much more water vapor to be distilled and turned into "pure" water. This is the same way Mother Nature produces rain. Evaporation of lake, river and ocean water occurs, then the condensation of the vapor falls as rain, snow, dew, fog or hail (thunk!). The reflector is also a great way to increase the output of the hot water heater, and to give it much better performance in the winter, especially with the low angle of sunshine.

Drill a hole and push a pipe of some sort through the top of the 2x4 and over and around the plastic so it still holds water. Be sure to use silicon caulk to seal the pipe and hole. Otherwise, the water vapor will leak out and not go into your condenser tubing. This output tube can be PVC, copper, iron and even some other types of flexible tubing (garden hose). The condenser would work best if it was copper, but even plastic tubing will work. The job of the tubing is to give up the heat of the water vapor and thus condense the water. If plastic is used, more of it will be needed. If a water cooler is not used, then more tubing in the open air will be needed. This page is not a "how to," but illustrates the *principles* to follow for making a desalination unit. *Get the water hot, get the vapor out, cool the vapor, and drink the water.*

Door and Glass Hot Water Heater With Reflector

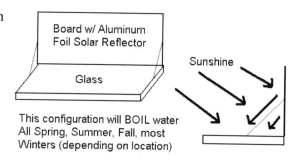

This configuration will BOIL water All Spring, Summer, Fall, most Winters (depending on location)

End Section Drawing of Glass/Door Solar Water Heater With Water Vapor Outlet Pipe

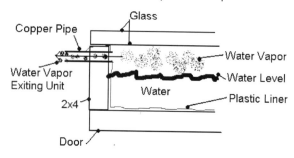

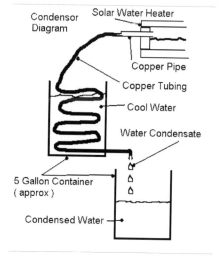

Condensor Diagram

[21]

http://www.solarcooking.org

Solar Cooking International is really an outstanding organization devoted to helping promote solar cooking around the world. This wonderful organization seems to be free from political and environmental motivations, and simply dedicated to helping of people. Their website is a wealth of plans, drawings, photos, and descriptions of solar cookers people have made around the world. This is an excellent place to get free information on solar cooking (which is a close cousin to solar heating). With the free glass, mirror and cardboard sources we have outlined in this book combined with the documentation on this website, there is no end to the number of projects and experiments that can be done for education, experimentation and even to the extent of starting very valid businesses. Make sure you look at the "Cook It" solar oven. It is 100% card board and aluminum foil, and can be made in an hour.

http://www.solarcooking.org/cookit.htm

http://www.ece.vill.edu/~nick

Since about 1995, Nick Pine has been answering any and all questions regarding heating, cooling, energy, and especially solar energy for heating and cooling through his "Nick Pine" web page and Usenet postings. His form and style of writing, and his explanations of mathematics, are nothing short of role model in quality. His archive of Usenet (newsgroup) postings on his website is a treasure trove of solar energy advice. Solarcooking.org will help you make a box that gets hot. Nick Pine's info will help you take a box that gets hot and use it to heat your house. Anyone who really wants to learn solar energy/energy/thermodynamics and more would be a lazy fool not to read everything Nick writes on a regular basis.

Nick Pine's email tagline describes himself as: Computer simulation and modeling. High performance, low cost, solar heating and cogeneration system design. BSEE, MSEE. Senior Member, IEEE. Registered US Patent Agent. Web site: http://www.ece.vill.edu/~nick

http://www.redrok.com

A great website run by a great and crazy guy who loves high temperature solar energy and many things associated with it. Duane's site is a large database of subjects with a large list of links to every energy subject you can think of on the web. The links are well maintained, and removed and updated on a regular basis. I only have THREE links to anyone else in this entire book on the subject of solar energy. Do you know why? They are the only ones that are really worth a darn. They're here because of their extreme EXCELLENCE.

Wisdom that Clemente Mesa taught myself and many others.

For all of you kids in school, college, or out of college, your learning JUST BEGINS when you leave school. It is not the end of learning; it is just the start. *Learning is a personal exercise that is to done DAILY by the individual.* It is up to YOU to teach yourself, to BUY your books, to take classes, to try experiments. This is on YOUR TIME. It is NOT the duty of your company to fund your education or books. It is YOUR DUTY to YOURSELF to do this. Everyday the gazelle must wake up and run a little faster to keep ahead of the lion. Every day the lion must wake up and run a little faster to catch the gazelle. One of these animals is either going to get eaten or is going to starve. Education, industry, and science are the same way for YOUR position. Evolve or die. Learn, or get replaced by someone better.

The Solar Puddle
A new water pasteurization technique for large amounts of water. *By Dr. Dale Andreatta, Derek Yegian*

The lack of clean drinking water is a major health problem in the developing world. To reduce this health risk, ways of producing clean water at an affordable cost are needed. People need to be educated about germs and sanitation, lest they accidentally re-contaminate their clean drinking water. Recently, several of us at the University of California at Berkeley have attacked the first of these requirements. Previous issues of this newsletter have included stories about our water pasteurization indicator and our flow-through water pasteurizers based on a design by PAX World Service. In this article, we describe a new low-cost device that pasteurizes water. For those not familiar with the pasteurization process, if water is heated to 149°F (65°C) for about six minutes, all the germs, viruses, and parasites that cause disease in humans are killed, including cholera and hepatitis A and B. This is similar to what is done with milk and other beverages. It is not necessary to boil the water as many people believe. Pasteurization is not the only way to decontaminate drinking water, but pasteurization is particularly easy to scale down so the initial cost is low. The new device is called a solar puddle, and it is essentially a puddle in a greenhouse. One form of the solar puddle is sketched in the figure on the following page, though many variations are possible.

One begins by digging a shallow pit about four inches deep. The test device was a "family-size" unit, about 3.5 by 3.5 feet, but the puddle could be made larger or smaller. If the puddle is made larger, there is more water to pasteurize, but there is also proportionately more sunshine collected. The pit is filled with two to four inches of solid insulation. We used wadded paper, but straw, grass, leaves, or twigs could be used. This layer of insulation should be made flat, except for a low spot in one corner of the puddle. Put a layer of clear plastic and then a layer of black plastic over the insulation with the edges of the plastic extending up and out of the pit. Two layers are used in case one develops a small leak. We used inexpensive polyethylene from a hardware store, though special UV stabilized plastic would last longer. Put in some water and flatten out the insulation so that the water depth is even to within about a half inch throughout the puddle, except in the trough which should be about one inch deeper than the rest. Put in more water so that the average depth is one to three inches, depending on how much sunshine is expected. A pasteurization indicator (available from Solar Cookers International at 916/455-4499) should go in this trough since this is where the coolest water will collect. Put a layer of clear plastic over the water, again with the edges extending beyond the edges extending beyond the edges of the pit. Form an insulating air gap by putting one or more spacers on top of the third layer of plastic (large wads of paper will do) and putting down a fourth layer of plastic, which must also be clear. The thickness of the air gap should be two inches or more. Pile dirt or rocks on the edges of the plastic sheets to hold them down. The puddle is drained by siphoning the water out, placing the siphon in the trough and holding it down by a rock or weight. If the bottom of the puddle is flat, well over ninety percent of the water can be siphoned out.

Once the puddle is built, it would be used by adding water each day, either by folding back the top two layers of plastic in one corner and adding water by bucket, or by using a fill siphon. The fill siphon should NOT be the same siphon that is used to drain the puddle, as the fill siphon is re-contaminated each day, while the drain siphon MUST REMAIN CLEAN. Once in place, the drain siphon should be left in place for the life of the puddle.

The only expensive materials used to make the puddle are a pasteurization indicator (about $2 for the size tested). All of these items are easily transportable, so the solar puddle might be an excellent option for a refugee camp if the expertise were available for setting them up. Many tests were done in the spring and summer of this year in Berkeley, California. On days with good sunshine, the required

[23]

temperature was achieved even with seventeen gallons of water (two and a half inch depth). About one gallon is the minimum daily requirement per person for drinking, brushing one's teeth, and dish washing. With thinner water layers, higher temperatures can be reached. With six gallons (one inch depth), 176°F was achieved on one day. The device seems to work even under conditions that are not ideal. Condensation in the top layer of plastic doesn't seem to be a problem, though if one gets a lot of condensation, the top layer should be pulled back to let the condensation evaporate. Small holes in the top layers don't make much difference. The device works in wind, or if the bottom insulation is damp. Water temperature is uniform throughout the puddle to within 2°F.

After some months, the top plastic layers weaken under the combined effects of sun and heat. They have to be replaced, but this can be minimized by avoiding hot spots. Another option would be to use a grade of plastic that is more resistant to sunlight. The two bottom layers of plastic tend to form tiny tears unless one is very careful in handling them, (that is why there are two layers on the bottom). A tiny hole may let a little water through and dampen the solid insulation, but this is not a big problem.

There are many variations of the solar puddle. We've been able to put the top layer of plastic into a tent-like arrangement that sheds rain. This would be good in a place that gets frequent brief showers. Adding a second insulating layer of air makes the device work even better, though this adds the cost of an extra layer of plastic. As mentioned, the device can cover a larger or smaller area if more or less water is desired. One could make a water heater by roughly tripling the amount of water so that the maximum temperature was only 120°F or so, and this water would stay warm well into the evening hours. This water wouldn't be pasteurized though. One could help solve the problem of dirty water vessels by putting drinking cups into the solar puddle and pasteurizing them along with the water. The solar puddle could possibly cook foods like rice on an emergency basis, perhaps in a refugee camp.

Dale Andreatta can be contacted at **dandreatta@seaohio.com,** *or contact Derek Yegian at:* **dtyegian@lbl.gov** *or Dr. Dale Andreatta, S. E. A. Inc., 7349 Worthington-Galena Road, Columbus, OH 43085. Telephone (614) 888-4160, or FAX (614) 885-8014. Reprinted with permission.*

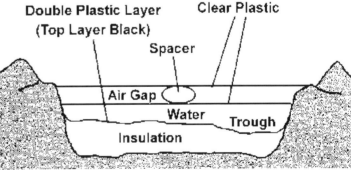

FREE FRESNEL LENSES (big ones)

(pronounced fra'nel)

The fresnel lens in modern manufacturing is a piece of clear plastic sheet with very fine grooves in the surface. It has the effect of magnification, and thus the concentration of light. These lenses are widely used in the front screens of big screen TV sets, usually with two sheets in the front. One lens has fresnel grooves in it while the other may have vertical grooves. You want the one with the fresnel or circular grooves. In the photo below, you see one pictured next to a bike tire for size reference. It actually has a piece cut out of it on its bottom left, but it still works great. The photo to the upper right shows a piece of wood in flames instantly after the Michigan summer sunshine is focused on the wood with the lens pictured below. Many times, a distinctive 'POP" can be heard as the light is put on the wood in maximum focus. This is actually the hydrogen molecule that was part of the organic cellulose molecule (roughly $C_6H_{10}O_5$) being thermally disassociated and instantly ignited as the 3000°F+ sunshine is put on the wood.

I get my lenses for FREE from TV repair shops. Look in the yellow pages and find ones that repair big screen TV's. Ask for "screens" that are scratched, marred, or damaged. These are normally thrown away. Good ones from broken TV's are saved for replacement parts for other TV's that are being fixed. The scratched ones are thrown in the dumpster. One shop saves three or four a month for me.

Sunshine is a very "diffuse" energy, meaning it is spread out. The concentration of the sunshine raises the "thermal quality" of the heat. Higher temperature means higher quality heat. The temperatures reached with a fresnel lens can be used to melt metal, especially aluminum and zinc. A well designed furnace with excellent insulation, good solar tracking, and focus will melt iron. It can be used to do biomass gasification, heat water, heat other gasses to make energy from the expansion of the gases (Sterling Engines). The fresnel lens works kind of opposite of parabolic dish. Both achieve the same result, but the fresnel focuses behind the lens and a parabolic system focuses in front of the dish. A fresnel lens is a tool not to be over looked in a person's experimentation and education in solar energy. The high temperature comes at a price. Precise tracking and focus must be done, but the resulting free high temperature heat is worth the effort.

These lenses are commonly sold through Edmond Scientific and other catalogs for between $75 and $150 each (brand new, not scratched). I prefer the scratched ones that I get for free.

CHEAP FRESNEL LENES (small ones)

One of my favorite sheet magnifiers is a seven by ten inch, very thin sheet magnifier that I got at Office Max or Office Depot. They cost about $8 each. Friends and visitors taking a tour of my labs always marvel at how fast a fire can be started with one of these small sheet magnifiers (fresnel lens). Most of the time, the fire starts instantly, especially on newspaper. It will make flames leap off of wood as well, just like the larger fresnel lenses described in this book.

Missionary friends of mine are interested in practicality of these sheet magnifiers. In many parts of the world, matches are so scarce or comparatively expensive that people will take ONE match from a small "book" of matches and rip it into six different pieces. One match is now six and can now start six different fires. (Try this yourself: separate the paper of the match in half, then rip the halves into three pieces each).

These sheet magnifiers can be found at most office supply stores such as Staples, Office Max and Office Depot. The magnifiers available in these stores are usually seven by ten inches, and are made of hard plastic. The lenses we supply are a very thin and flexible plastic that can be bent and rolled without damaging the lens. These will not break like the hard plastic ones in the office stores. In the year 2002, these became available at **http://www.KnowledgePubications.com** at a cost of $4.95 each. Quantity discounts are available.

I highly suggest obtaining some of these lenses and doing experiments. These are NOT like the little magnifying lens you played with as a child. Most newspaper will burst into flames (especially the dark areas of the paper). This will happen even in winter sunshine in Michigan. Make sure the lens is held PERPENDICULAR to the sunshine, and make a very fine focus. It takes about one minute of practice but it is really easy. BE CAREFUL!! One customer was reading the

writing on the clear wrapping around the lens while driving his car down the road. His car had a sun roof, and the sun was at the right angle. The lens was the right distance from his leg, and he set his pants on fire! This is a true story. With proper focusing, this lens will create temperatures in excess of 3000°F.

A small fresnel lens starting newspaper on fire on February 2nd, 2002, in Michigan.

FREE INSULATION AND MORE

Metal surfaced, 1 3/4 inch foam core doors, FREE. Pictured here are a total of ten foam core doors that I got for free. Seven are leaning up against my Dodge Dakota and three more are in the bed of the truck. I got all these for FREE, and more are on the way. They did not come from a door manufacturer, but from a company that buys the brand new doors by the truck load everyday, and then cuts knockouts (sections) from the door in order to insert decorative glass, shiny brass handles and other accouterments. The doors I got are "slightly" marred or damaged, but do not affect its insulation value for me. I was hard pressed to even find the defects. I called door manufacturers and installers, but the best type of business I found was the door "wholesaler." Again, they modify the base door and sell these to other wholesale and construction companies. These little panels are the "knock outs" from new doors. A large router cuts through the metal skin and foam, and then the glass is inserted. The knockout can be as big as seventy-five percent of the door if that door is going to have a large piece of glass in its center. Earlier photos of doors with mostly glass are USED, removed doors that I got from the glass company, which I also got the normal sliding glass door glass from. For free doors, knockouts and doors with glass in them, check with glass and mirror shops, door manufacturers, door wholesalers, and door sales companies. It takes some phone calls, but it did not take me long to start getting more doors, knockouts, and glass than I could handle. And, it was all for FREE. Smaller knockouts go in my attic for added insulation. A friend in Texas built an entire little café from nothing but door knockouts...floors, walls and roof. Hey, go to Conger's Café in Hereford, Texas, for some great food!

Mass Manufactured Refrigeration Components for Ice Making and Air Conditioning.

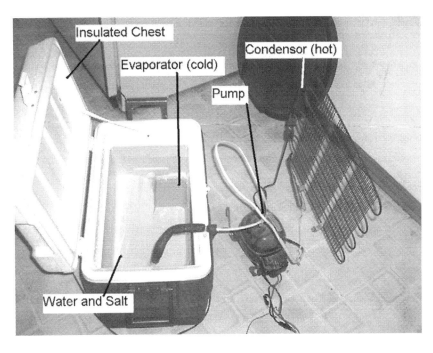

You cannot build a refrigeration system cheaper than you can buy a new one in the form of a refrigerator on sale in a big store. However, you can get a refrigerator for free from places that reclaim the refrigerant before a refrigerator/freezer can be thrown away. They are often HAPPY to have you take the refrigerator away instead of them having to remove the refrigerant oil and send the unit to the junk yard (and they still charge the guy who wanted to dispose of the refrigerator). I get my FREE refrigerators from my City Recycling center. People throw away working refrigerators all the time.

I had a small, working, under the table refrigerator, the type you get for less than $100, which I took apart. I stripped away the entire cabinet and refrigerator shell and took out the condenser, pump and evaporator. The evaporator is the part that gets cold inside the refrigerator, while the pump moves the refrigerant. The condenser is the part that gets hot on the back of the refrigerator (this is a heat pump, and it pumps heat from inside the refrigerator to the outside of the refrigerator). The cold evaporator gets to -5°F in a well insulated container (which the original refrigerator is NOT).

I used a "5 Day Ice Cooler" for my initial experiments, but you can make an insulated container with wood and Styrofoam as shown in this book for making solar ovens and hot water heaters. Just line it with plastic to hold the water, and two inches of foam insulation around the unit. Insulation is the secret here.

Most people think of refrigerators as being power hungry, but these little units are very efficient and can be made even more efficient. This little unit draws ONLY ninety-three watts. It draws six hundred watts for about a half second on start up, but then settles down to ninety-three watts. I have run mine on a $28 four hundred-watt inverter (eight hundred-watt surge) with success.

The classic one hundred year old method of making ice (other than cutting it out of a lake) is to use mechanical refrigeration of some type (a refrigerator is mechanical refrigeration), and to cool water and salt (brine) to as low a temperature as possible. In our example here, it gets cooled to minus five degrees Fahrenheit. That's five BELOW zero (-5°F).

To make the brine, just take tap water and salt and mix it up. The salt is available from warehouse stores (Costco/Sam's) and restaurant supply stores (Gordon Food Service GFS) for about $3 for twenty-five pounds. Use a paint mixer on the end of a drill to mix the salt into the water. Stop adding salt when the water will not hold any more salt (you'll set it on the bottom and it won't dissolve). This is called a saturated salt solution.

When the brine is this cold, insert a container of fresh water to be frozen. Make sure the brine does not get in the bucket holding the fresh water. A plastic or a metal pail can be used. Most people don't know that really thin plastics conduct heat about as well as metal does. Plastic bags of fresh water, plastic pails, five gallon pails, and plastic "tubs" can all be used. These can have open tops or be sealed. A bucket of fresh water will "float" in salt water or brine. Brine has a higher density than the fresh water. This is the same reason that oil and other things float on top of water. Just don't let the brine get in the fresh water to be frozen if this is going to be used for ice cubes. Why use salt water? Why not just make ice cubes like one does in their home freezer? Air is an insulator, and it does NOT conduct heat very well. The object here is to freeze a bunch of water into ice with the lowest amount of energy. Someone trying to do this with solar panels does not have a surplus of energy. Cold refrigerant to metal (the evaporator), to brine, to plastic (the bucket), to fresh water, transfers heat MUCH better than metal to air, to plastic, and to water. If

you don't believe me, put your hand in a freezer and see how long you can keep it there. Next, put your hand in the -5°F brine. You'll know the meaning of PAIN in the -5°F brine. In the photo, Kim is holding ice that was made in a $1, three gallon plastic pail. Samantha is holding the pail, although you can only see the top of it. Three gallons of ice weighs about twenty-four pounds, and it took about two hours to freeze solid. Freezing bags of "flat" water works faster because ice is a less thermally conductive than water. It takes more time to freeze the ice in the center of the bucket. Flat and narrow is the best "shape" to freeze something in. Using a pump or agitator to move the brine around will also decrease the needed freezing time.

Other parts of this book will cover "chemical" cooling and ice making. However, the method above is the smallest and lightest way of making ice. It requires electricity or rotary horsepower of some kind to move the compressor, but this method can't be beat for its efficiency, size, and cost..."IF" you have the electricity.

Other parts of this book will talk about "microclimating" for the purposes of cooling a sleeping area or person. The cold brine or fresh water made by this method can be circulated by a small pump through a heat exchanger (such as an automotive heater core from the dash of a car), while air is blown through the heater core for the purpose of cooling a tent, room, or person.

Can you have ICE and Hot Water at the same time? Yes! This is easy, and you can make twice the amount of ice at the same time. Remember that we said that air is an insulator and a poor conductor of heat? While the evaporator is in the liquid brine, the condenser is in the air. The more efficient the heat is transferred, the more efficient the unit. Putting the condenser in a pool of water that can give up its heat to the atmosphere will increase the COP, or Coefficient Of Performance. COP is a measurement of how much "cold" a unit makes (or pumps) for X amount of energy. Increasing the heat transfer will not lower the pump load, but can DOUBLE the amount of ice that is made with the 93 watts of electric power my pump uses. You'll make the same amount of ice twice as fast AND have extra HOT water. Don't let the "hot" water get much above 110°F, or you'll start lowering your COP. That is still nice bath water or a source of heat when it is cold.

[29]

Make Energy, Make Ice, Make Money.

The economics of energy are such that the last thing you would want to do is to sell the energy to the grid. The grid is the lowest price there is. The best thing is to use your own energy to make a product of higher value. Only when there is a surplus of energy would you "dump" it to the grid. Keep in mind that I am NOT talking photovoltaic panels in this example. There is no economics in PV panels except for the economics of you paying too much for a product.

I have an excellent example of the economics of energy. A good friend of mine in Haiti has taken it upon himself to feed many thousands of people a day. He sets up and runs churches and orphanages, and will help anyone. Haiti is a very poor country with little or no resources. There is nothing to manufacture, and nothing to export. It does have an abundance of sunshine, but we'll get to that in a bit.

The capital city of Haiti has electricity for MAYBE two hours a day, sometime around two AM, if that. It is generally hot in Port-Au-Prince and there is always a demand for ice. Not much ice is made in Haiti. I sat down with Stenyo and did the economics. By STARTING him with a surplus, very efficient diesel engine/ electricity generation system. By using cheap or free refrigeration components, we could help him make ice and make money to help feed people. The economics of it are such that $1.50 to $2.50 in diesel fuel would make thirty to thirty-five dollars of ice. After getting him up and running using diesel fuel (which IS available on a "regular" basis), eventually we could move him over to solar

ice making. Solar ultimately has better economics but is much more complicated, physically large with weights in the tons. The $300 diesel engine we got was a 3HP Lister (runs 20,000+ hours), a pair of deep cycle batteries as a load leveling filter ($200), a large diesel truck alternator optimized for max output at low RPM ($250), and a 1500-watt inverter ($225). The refrigeration components would be similar to those on the previous page. Of course, we would build our own containers from plywood, plastic, and foam to hold the brine, and cool the condenser with water to increase the ice making efficiency. To make an even higher dollar item, all you need to do is to take the ice, turn it into a snow cone, put flavor on it, and sell it at a fair. They aren't going to sell snow cones in Haiti, but this is an example of the economics of energy and how it relates to manufacturing.

The generator you see pictured is a " Dual Series Hybrid Diesel/ Gasoline Electric Generator." It is very similar in concept to a hybrid electric vehicle (which I am NOT a fan of). The inverter can generate 120V AC from either the batteries or the generator load leveled through the batteries. The batteries can be recharged by the generator and by the truck alternator and electrical system. The truck can also power the inverter. This unit has traveled with me for about 30,000 miles. It was on a 10,000-mile trip around the USA, and it ran my 600-watt air conditioner every night. It used about one gallon of diesel for every six hours of air conditioner operation. The air conditioner was keeping the trailer cool in a 100°F+ ambient environment in the hot, arid southwest of the United States.

Diesel engines hold the world record for efficiency for a mass-produced chemical combustion to rotary horsepower device. Many of the newer diesel engines (DI Diesels) run at a higher brake thermal efficiency than most fuel cells. Want a vehicle MORE efficient than a fuel cell vehicle? Buy a new VW with a Turbo Diesel.

Water to Air Heat Exchange
Hot Water for Heating
Cold Water for Cooling.

In this book, we talk about ways of making materials HOT and COLD. One of those materials is WATER, H2O. We are cooling, chilling, or freezing water and heating or boiling water. Many times, we want to use our hot or cold water for heating or cooling. Although solar energy is usually best used in heating a house by heating and moving air, many times heat for the night will be stored in water. Getting heat from the water into the house or sleeping area is also one of the best ways for storing "cold" for cooling during the day. Many times, we'll make "cold" at night and use it during the day the same we make "hot" during the day and use it at night.

I'm going to start this section with an example of using a heat exchanger for cooling the house.

How can you cool the house by watering your grass with warm water? It is easily done by putting heat into the water before it goes on the grass. I soldered two garden hose spigots (with valves) and a regular on/off valve into the 3/4 inch copper water line in my house. This is the line that comes from the main and feeds the rest of the house. The city or well water that comes into your house is generally near the Earth average temperature (eight to fifty feet down) of about 55°F. This will vary by how deep your water line is, and how far it runs near the surface of the ground to your house. In Michigan, my water temp is 55°F in the winter and about 62°F (at most) in the summer. I really like blowing 63°F air into my house on a hot 85, 90, or 95°F degree day.

Normal Mode:
In normal operation, both of the hose valves are CLOSED and the center valve is OPEN. This allows water to flow through the house normally with no cooling.

Cooling Mode:
If you have well water, you can do this more economically all day long by moving water UP one well and then DOWN another well. If I tried to run my unit all day long for every room in the house, I'd have a water bill that would be a little expensive. However, there is no reason for me to put perfectly good cold water on the grass when it will take warm water just as easily.

When I go to water my lawn in the summertime, I turn OFF the center valve (which actually would stop all of the water going to the house), and open up the valves that bypass the center valve, sending water through a hose. This goes through a heat exchanger blowing cold air into the room, while the "warmer" water goes back into the house water pipe through the second hose and valve.

The heat exchanger you see is one from a large van. It is the auxiliary heater used to keep

[31]

people warm in the back of the vehicle. It is just a heat exchanger, and heat exchangers can heat and cool. In this case, we are moving cold water through it while moving warm air in one side and cooler air out the other side. You can find one of these at a junkyard pretty cheap. This one already has a nice blower built into it, and it really blows a lot of air. I use a 12-volt power supply to run the blower (or you can use solar panels and/or batteries). Sometimes, I have my free solar panels (covered elsewhere in this book) power the blower directly as the water flows through the unit. It blows cool air in my work area. If a cloud passes over, I can hear the blower go up and down (but I need less cooling anyway when it gets cloudy). Yes, I've used this for many hundreds of hours (summer of 2002) before I put it in this book.

How effective is this unit? How much cooling can it do? It dumps over 40,000 BTU's per hour of heat into the rear of a vehicle. In a cooling mode, we won't do that much. But, Trevor Babcock did a series of experiments on this for me, and it did over 3800 BTU's per hour of cooling. This was NOT optimized, but was just running quick and dirty. We had WAY too much water flow, over six gallons per minute. This unit really wants to run at a lower water flow rate (two gallons per minute), and a high airflow rate. If it runs at two gallons per minute, and there are 8.3 lbs of water in a gallon, and sixty minutes in an hour, and we raise the temperature of the water from 60F to 65F, then this will do: 8.3lbs/gal x 2gal/min = 16.6 lbs/min and 16.6lbs/min x 60min/hr = 996lbs/hr.

It takes one BTU to raise one pound of water one degree Fahrenheit, so if we raise 996 pounds of water five degrees Fahrenheit, then 996lbs/hr x 5 degrees F = 4980 BTU's/HR of cooling. This is the same as a 5000 BTU, $120 window air conditioner, and you get this cooling for FREE. You were going to

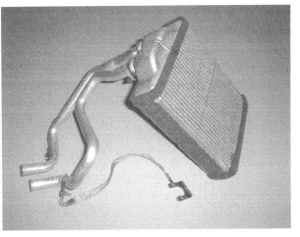

water the grass anyway, so why not cool the room at the same time? With this system any water use can help you cool your home. Now imagine if you use eight gallons per minute instead of two gallons per minute. That's 20,000 BTU's of cooling, FREE. The air coming out of the unit will be near the warmest temperature of your water leaving the unit. In this example the unit would be flowing 65°F air into the room.

If the larger heat exchanger I was showing is hard to find, you'll have an easier time finding this smaller one that goes in the dash of a car. This unit is about the size of a cigar box and is more suited for blowing cold air onto a person while sleeping using small fans and blowers. Don't underestimate this unit. By blowing 250CFM (cubic feet per minute) of air through it, you can cool an entire room very quickly. I cooled my 12 x 12 foot bedroom from 85°F to 72°F in about forty-five minutes with this very heater core, but I had a bigger blower. This does not have to operate with a large, power hungry blower. We'll be showing how to do microclimating work in the book. For this, you can use a much lower water flow rate through the unit (one tenth to one half gallon per minute), and a small blower at 10, 20, or 30CFM. This is actually a "muffin" fan from a computer power supply. It runs on 120V AC, and you can use a light dimmer to control its speed. To make the little blower more effective,

Make a duct (box) between the fan and the heater core with cardboard, hard plastic or plastic sheeting or wood to force all of the air through all of the heater core.

separate the two units using cardboard, plastic, and duct tape or liquid nails to form a shroud between the blower and the heater core. This moves air through the entire heater core. Muffin fans vary greatly in their output. The ones that are quieter are down around 10-30CFM, while the noisier ones are around 100CFM. Of course, this rating is in the open with little restriction. The heater core provides a restriction, depending on which one you have, what the tube and fins spacing is used, etc. I'd rather have a 100CFM muffin fan and put a 120-volt light dimmer control on it to adjust the speed than to have one that is too small. It does not matter how much cold water there is flowing through the heater core if you don't have enough airflow. It will not cool your room or space. In technical terms, it is stated as the Q of the air being equal to the Q of the water. This means that the cooling absorbed into the air must equal the heat that went into the water. If you want to understand how everything works around you, people, trees, cars, the sun, etc., then study thermodynamics and heat transfer. Your life will never be boring.

**GETTING ABSURD
(but interesting)
WITH USING THE WATER.**

I did a crazy experiment with the cooling water on the previous page. I took the cold water from the water line (to water the lawn) and used the water to cool the house. Then I ran the water to a hose sprinkler on the roof of my house. The water cooled the black shingles on top of the hose (thus removing solar heat input to my house that needed to be cooled). The warmer water ran into the gutters on the roof, and I directed the water down to the condenser of an air conditioner I had running in my main den. The water on the condenser of the air conditioner improved the heat removal from the condenser and thus raised the COP (coefficient of performance) of my air conditioner. I was making more cold for the same amount of electricity. I then ran the much warmer water from the bottom of the air conditioner through some pipes and conduits to the grass, and finally the grass was watered. This was an experiment, and it worked, but it was a little too...well...I didn't need the neighbors laughing that hard at me. It would have taken considerable effort to make this a permanent part of the house.

ENERGY CASCADE

The French solar energy pioneer, Trombe, considered the use of solar energy to heat water to make steam that could turn a turbine, which in turn would make electricity. This was a waste when the same energy could melt steel. This is true. You can take 4000°F+ solar energy and melt iron (2300°F), use the iron to melt brass (1800°F), use the brass to melt aluminum (1200°F), use the aluminum to melt zinc (900°F), use the zinc to melt lead (600°F), and use the lead to heat the water to make steam to turn the turbine to make electricity.

Now there is a thought that will keep you up at night thinking.

Steam Distillation; Salt Water to Fresh Water "Desalination"

This unit is a variation of the solar hot water heater already documented in this book. This unit has the ability to vaporize the water in salt water and to condense and move those fresh water vapors and/or the fresh water out of the unit.

This is not only important for turning salt water into drinking water (distilled water), but also for water pasteurization purposes (see the solar puddle article). Further, the solar distillation unit will be a crucial part of our system for making ice via chemical methods and very important for the harvesting of moisture (water) from the air.

Like the other solar hot water heaters in this book, this is a double-layered glass (sliding glass door glass) over 2x4's and plastic (for holding the water) sitting on a door (for insulation). Copper was added for condensing the steam.

I used a half inch copper pipe, but three-quarter inch could have been used. Plastic or PVC pipe could have also been used. I used copper because it conducts heat better than PVC pipe, but PVC is cheaper and easier to work with.

First, make sure the unit is level. Then add water to the unit, making sure you don't get water in the STEAM PIPE. It can easily hold fifteen gallons of water.

The steam in pipe is about one-

The Completed Unit

Close up of the Steam In and Water Out

Copper pipes and wood under the black plastic and glass

Close up of the Steam In pipe, use silicone caulk to seal this to the plastic.

quarter of an inch below the 2x4-inch edge and the glass. Water vapor/steam will form from the water being solar heated between the top of the water and the glass. The water does NOT have to be at 212°F (boiling) for this to happen. As the water gets hotter, a slight pressure will build up. The water vapor will then exit through the STEAM IN tube. When it flows down the tube, it will lose its' heat through the copper tube and black plastic and give it up to the water. When the water loses enough heat (975 BTU's per pound), it will go from a vapor state back to a liquid state. This is called a "Double Acting" distillation unit because the heat used to vaporize the water gets put back into the water being heated. The water will condense in the copper tube and flow out as water. IF enough solar heat is added, like with a reflector, or if it is hot enough outside, all of the water may NOT condense in the pipe, and steam may escape. If this occurs, then a second condenser will be needed (see the previous articles on water desalination/distillation).

I used about twenty feet of half-inch copper pipe in the heat exchanger. Each ten-foot "stick" cost about $4 at Home Depot. It was cut with a tubing cutter and soldered together with a propane torch (a tutorial on soldering tubing is beyond this book, but it is easy enough to ask the guys at your hardware store). Depending on your location, you can use MORE or LESS copper pipe. Plastic piping is also an option. If you have water vapor escaping on a regular basis, then you'll want more pipe. This unit easily got up to 190°F on a clear, April day in Michigan (with no reflectors, just the glass laying flat). When the water temp gets this hot, it will be very hard for the 190°F steam vapor to transfer enough heat to surrounding water to fully condense, an additional condenser will be needed.

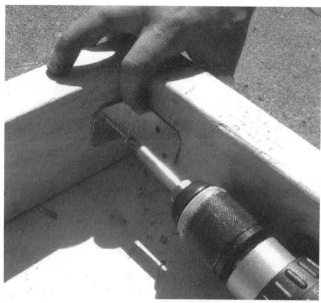

METAL CORNERS
To fasten the wood together on this unit, I used metal corners from Home Depot. The corners cost about fifty cents each and took a total of two screws. I found this easier than screwing the wood together, but that is still an option. Even nailing the wood together is an acceptable option. The principle is NOT to follow this book STEP BY STEP, but the principle is to USE WHAT YOU HAVE.

...and the water is deep, too...
I used 2x4-inch wood for the sides, but if you wanted to hold MORE water then six inches, eight, ten, or twelve-inch wood could be used. You'll have to make the corners more secure and you might want to screw it to the bottom board/insulation, but this is a viable option. It will take longer to heat up, but you might not need to add water in the middle of the day.

DON'T RUN OUT OF WATER
Do NOT run this unit out of water. The plastic sheet will MELT and get holes when the unit runs out of water. For a long life unit that does not require attention, you might want to consider making the inside material sheet metal that is sealed with silicone or something else. For doing experiments and homework, the black plastic sheeting is great way to start. If you melt some plastic, don't worry about it. Learn from the experiment and make it better with what you have available.

YOUR ADDITIONS TO THIS
To make this more of an automatic system, a person should add a float switch (like from a toilet) to automatically fill the unit with water when it gets low. This would require adding a copper tube to add water to the unit. Depending on the double layer glass you are using, you may or may NOT have to seal the glass to the plastic and wood. For our work, I did not need to do this. For a permanent instillation, I would seal the glass and plastic to the wood. Silicone caulk will work fine.

*** IMPORTANT ***
PRINCIPLES IN THIS UNIT for MAKING ICE and COLD
Keep in mind the PRINCIPLES of how this unit works. Sunshine on glass over water with insulation drives the water away in the form of steam and leaves everything else behind. It will leave bugs, rocks, salt, minerals and everything else in the unit. Put in seawater and let it run and you will have only salt left in the bottom. We will be using this PRINCIPLE to recycle and reuse our chemicals (salts) for making solar ice and solar refrigeration and other fun solar chemistry.

SUNSHINE TO DOLLARS DVD
Much of the construction of this unit is documented on the Sunshine to Dollars DVD available at **www.KnowledgePublcations.com**

HOUSE CONSTRUCTION
Brain-dead Simple vs. Brain-dead Stupid.

I'm going to talk about new construction and solar energy, and under NO TIME during this am I talking about solar photovoltaic energy. Real solar energy is solar thermal energy.

Construction companies, their customers, and the whole industry are passing up economic opportunities everyday, and flushing dollars down the toilet. By not integrating year 2003+ mass manufacturing of plastics, glass, and metal into modern construction, they are acting like a teenager turning down an eight-year scholarship to a university.

Why is this not being done? Because "YOU ARE NOT DOING IT." You, the reader, sitting there on the couch and reading this book, are the reason nothing is being accomplished. YOU are not doing it. Forget saying "they's" and "them's" (such as, " Why aren't 'THEY' doing it?"). There is absolutely NO reason anyone with the desire cannot implement many of these items into a future house construction.

It is at the time of construction that many of these best practices should be implemented. I'm not talking real expense here, and some of the return on investment can take less than a year. Some of the methods SAVE you money on construction. It can actually be cheaper to put tempered glass on a roof than it is to use plywood, tar paper and shingles.

LOOK AT THAT SURFACE AREA!

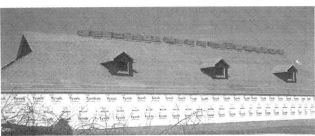

Look at the roof of the business pictured. The entire area above the wall line is all "unused attic." The southern exposure of this building is enough to heat and cool it all summer and winter. There is enough surface area there for it to heat and cool adjacent buildings. Those little additions to the roof with windows are only for appearance, money spent on form with no function. Look at the photograph of the windows in the house above. There is probably $5000 in window work, and yet $5000 could completely make this $350,000 house solar heated with a return on the money spent over a few Michigan winters (a typical house like this can have $200 per month heat bill, or a six month average of $1200 per year...making a four year return on investment). I did not even factor summertime solar cooling into this number.

Most new houses have enough North/South surface area to integrate a reasonable amount of solar for heating and cooling. All of the mass manufacturing and methods exist today to seamlessly integrate this with modern heating and air conditioning systems. I am not suggesting the replacement of current forced air furnaces and central air conditioning systems, but the augmentation of them with the economics of sunshine falling on the house all year round.

Sizing a solar heating/cooling system to make a house 100% independent becomes VERY costly. Supplementing the house with available sunshine becomes very economical. It is the minds and thoughts of people that have been polluted that has caused solar augmentation to be bypassed. All solar heating and cooling in an on-demand world with a hundred years of grid infrastructure does not make economic sense.

PUT SOLAR IN WHEN YOU BUILD.
This roof truss system on the right is just begging for some glass and heat passages to be integrated. A "Modern" building methods has these sections being quickly fabricated on the ground at the site, and then hoisted with a crane onto the house. At this time glass, additional wood and insulation with a few heating ducts can be as easily integrated as roofing plywood and tarpapers are put on a standard roof.

Construction companies dig holes and fill them with concrete to make a basement with lightning speed and efficiency. Don't ignore the discussion of storing solar heating and cooling in the attic, walls, and roof area of a house (which we recommend), when the traditional method of solar heat storage is a hole in the ground with rocks or bottles of water. All of the mechanisms are there to make thermal storage exist today in our modern basement building methods.

IT IS STILL 1930!!
We are building houses and turning down our free "Solar Economics Scholarships." It is the 21st century, and we are still building houses almost exactly the same way we did in the 1930's, with concrete, 2x4's, insulation, plaster, plywood and shingles. The biggest difference is that we now have power nail guns and other power tools instead of hand tools.

We still make a 2x4 frame, and put drywall on the inside and brick on the outside. Anyone making a thermally efficient house knows that you put the thermal mass (the bricks) on the INSIDE of the house, NOT the outside. We have world-class materials that look like bricks and give brick-like protection from the weather, but we still spend twenty man-days laying one brick at a time with mortar around a house. What a waste of money and human effort.

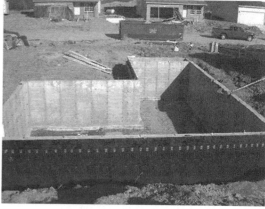

Really good 21st Century construction involves the use of Structurally Insulated Panels (SIPS) and Insulated Concrete Forms (ICF blocks). If you are going to build a house, at least look at this 1960's technology. Foam walls and shotcrete, and inflation forms with shotcrete are another great form of construction. We have ignored modern methods used in other businesses and ignored modern composite materials and METHODS just because this is the way we've been building houses since 1930. Most builders have their heads up their rear ends so they can stare at their pocketbooks from the inside out. Not Invented Here (NIH) syndrome and complacency are two additional reasons these methods are not widely used. YOU not doing it is another reason. Foam, plastics, wood composites, and filler reinforced concretes with new materials are all fields that are WIDE open, waiting for someone with vision and commitment. Fortunes on the scale of billions await those who undertake the mission. Your biggest obstacle are the people who could not find their rear end with both hands and who have fingers perpetually stuck up their noses.

UPDATES TO THIS BOOK and ENERGY PHILOSOPHY.

This book was born on January 3rd, 2002, when I sold the first sixteen-page version on eBAY. Since then, I have continually updated the book and kept on putting out a new version about every two months. This version is the seventh version of the book, and is the first one to have the solar cooling systems in it.

Through my professional life, I have always photo-documented the experiments and work that I did. This book was born from the photos and documentation of many of the projects I have done. I did not do experiments initially for the purpose of the book. It was actually the other way around.

As I now continue my solar experiments and work, I continue to take photos and to expand the book. The book gets expanded and taken into new area as one experiments leads to another. You will see several generations of solar heaters, distillation units, and ovens in the book, as one has grown into another and another etc. Each section of the book could actually be expanded into a whole book itself.

The solar experiments in this book are NOT what I do professionally. I do professional development work on solar energy systems that can supply the USA with all of the energy it needs for automotive transportation, heating, cooling, and electricity. The experiments I do for this book are for my personal amusement, and are my hobby. However, keep in mind that these experiments are illustrating principles behind solar energy, thermodynamics, and material science as well as energy and heat transfer. It also deals with modern manufacturing and other modern science methods. Real solar energy and solar thermal energy that can provide enough energy for everyone on the planet, whether there is six billion, ten billion, twenty billion, fifty billion, or more, all has its basis in this book. The experiments in this book are simpler and at lower temperatures than many of the "cutting-edge technology" methods we are doing development work on right now, but the PRINCIPLES are the SAME.

The energy field is exciting. It is growing, and is the single largest market in the world. It is responsible for the quality and quantity of human life and our technology advancement more than anything else. To limit energy is to kill human beings.

When I talk to people about the solar energy businesses and solar heating for homes and solar cooling, they say, "Yeah...look at all of the energy people can save."

WRONG It is NOT about saving energy. The methods I show and teach for you and your house, and for the future of man, are NOT for saving energy. It is for USING MORE ENERGY. We, as humans, will ALWAYS use MORE AND MORE energy every second of every minute of hour of every day, year, decade, and century. It cannot be stopped, and it is NOT bad. It is what keeps us alive and keeps us advancing. As man advances, he always improves himself. The two things that historically enable him are communications and energy. To stay at the same level of energy use for even one day is the same as reducing energy, and thus the people on the bottom of the energy ladder fall off and die.

So keep on experimenting and keep on thinking. As my dear friend and fellow instructor, Al Kargilils, says, "You must be a warrior poet."

More and newer versions of this book will be coming out every couple of months. In the winter, I add items about solar heating. In the summer, I add things about solar cooling. During the year, I add things about solar cooking, the uses of solar energy, and the needs for solar energy.

Hey...it's falling on your head all day, and it's free, so you might as well use it.

Also note, I am now documenting my experiments with video and there will be a *Sunshine to Dollars DVD* coming out soon with exciting and FUN video.

All my Best,
Steven E. Harris
http://www.StevenHarris.net

Civil Defense & Solar Ovens

Normally in a Solar Energy book, this is where someone will say something about foreign oil, US politics, and energy independence. This book won't address this in the aspects of solar energy and civil defense because it just does not matter.

Natural disasters and man-made disasters will befall us in the future. It can't be stopped. Hurricanes like Andrew and Katrina will make entire areas helpless for days and weeks, and people who hate the USA will do something far worse than Sept 11th that will kill millions of Americans. It won't be billions of dollars in damage, but trillions of dollars in damage to the economy.

I have been volunteering my time and working in the Emergency Services and Civil Defense field for almost twenty years now. I've contributed papers and ideas to the Center for Disease Control, Publish Health Service, FEMA, the US Air Force, US Special Forces, and other public and private institutions. I also teach simple home and family preparedness in seminars and classes and one on one.

I wrote earlier in the book that safe water, sewage removal, antibiotics, and abundant energy were the key reasons why we have six billion people living on the Earth in 2002. In disasters of epic scale, a population quickly loses water and energy, and people start to die in days.

A complete class on preparedness is well beyond the scope of this book. However, I do want to point out that a solar oven and some white flour, water, salt, and baking powder makes very nice biscuits and that water obtained from a river or lake is "safe" to drink after it has been heated above 160F in a solar oven.

For a group of people who have the mission to help others in a time of need, a large solar oven like the one in this book can bake one hundred loaves of bread in a day without using up very precious fuel.

It is smart to have methods of cooking and baking that do not require solar energy, but every day that you use the free solar energy falling on your head is a day of extra fuel you can use for other purposes.

For those of you who are prepared, or want to be prepared, please look into solar energy cooking as one of the tools you need for yourself and your family. Don't forget that you can use it to help other people in time of crisis.

Further Civil Defense information is on **www.StevenHarris.net**

(Photographs of the World Trade Center were taken by the author, Steven E. Harris)

About The Author

Steven E. Harris
Photograph courtesy of May Kearny

Project Destiny
- Solar photons to electrons through hydrogen.
- 95% off the shelf.
- No photovoltaic panels, no fuel cells.
- Made with aluminum, glass, iron, steel, copper, plastic, and ceramic.
- 100- year-old technology with 21st Century science, methods and

Steven Harris is a consultant in the energy field. He serves as Director of Operations and Technology for the American Hydrogen Association in the Midwest. After spending ten years in the Aero-Thermal Dynamics department of the Scientific Labs of Chrysler Corporation, where he was a pioneer member of the group that developed and implemented successful Speed-to-Market development concepts. Mr. Harris left his position to do full time work on the development and implementation of hydrogen, biomass, and solar-related energy systems.

Mr. Harris is currently working with Roy McAlister and others on Project Destiny, a solar hydrogen energy system. He is authoring an upcoming book, "The Positive Promotion of Hydrogen Energy, a Model for Success in an Economically Driven Market."

In addition to energy, Mr. Harris has a life long commitment to civil defense and the preparedness and protection of the American public. He teaches family preparedness and education regarding threats to the population.

Mr. Harris's Experience, Projects and a Consulting Portfolio can be found at: http://www.StevenHarris.Net.

Contact Steven Harris at:
h2fuel@mail.com

Or visit:

www.KnowledgePublications.com

SURVIVING THE BLACKOUT OF 2003
(8/14/2003)

Energy & Family Preparedness Tips, Tricks & True Stories of Experiencing the Adventure of the Disaster.

By Steven E. Harris
Author of Sunshine to Dollars,
Civil Defense Professional,
& Energy Consultant

http://www.StevenHarris.net
h2fuel@mail.com

(c)2003 KnowledgePublications.com
(permission for duplication or quotation must be licensed or requested)

ISBN: 978-1-60322-000-2

Version 1.3, Updated 11/03/2003

Ebook version available from
www.KnowledgePublications.com

I have Free Family Preparedness Classes in Audio MP3 format available at www.KnowledgePublications.com.
This class will enable you to make food at home from stuff that costs pennies at the grocery store . You can be eating in minutes, and it's so good that the kids will love it. Anyone can download the classes for free.

Fore more free stuff, also see:
www.BeforeTheStormHits.com
www.USAHomelanddefense.com
Www.NuclearSurvivalSkills.com

Copyright, 2006

By

www.KnowledgePublications.com

Stay Safe, Stay Informed, Stay Safe.

The Start of the Adventure - The Detroit Michigan Area.

This document will tell the personal adventure of the author, Steven Harris, through the blackout of 2003. It will chronicle some of my work with emergency services and how an energy expert and civil defense expert handled the adventure. Note: At this time, it is called the Blackout of 2003, with the power grid vulnerability, international terrorism and computer terrorism, it COULD become named the FIRST Blackout of 2003 or the SHORTEST Blackout of 2003.

It was about 4:14pm, I had just eaten a light lunch and was on the couch for a few minutes looking at the news, or the history channel, when the power failed. It came back on about four seconds later and stayed on for a few moments and then it went out and stayed out. It was Thursday August 14th, 2003.

There were no thunderstorms, no rain and it was a sunny clear day with a high pressure system located over / near Michigan. Why do I know this? Because I do solar research and development work. I always know when sunny days are occurring because I usually have tests running on solar ovens / heaters / solar coolers and other items. (I don't work on solar photovoltaic [PV], the worst thing that ever happened to the solar business).

I have a significant background of extensive training and work in the civil defense field, and the effects of nuclear weapons, chemical agents and biological terrorism on a civilian population. One of the key things a person with these types training ALWAYS does when the power fails is to turn on a battery radio / TV to see if there are any stations on the air. The other thing we do is to pick up the telephone and see if there was dial tone. Why do we do this?

If a large Soviet style nuclear device was detonated at high altitude it creates an Electro Magnetic Pulse (EMP) that would fry the majority of the non-hardened electronic circuits in the USA, this would include about 90% of the power grid. This is always a prelude to a full nuclear attack coming. So we always pick up the phone or turn on a radio to see if the power failure is just us or if it is much larger.

I hopped in my car and turned on the radio and half of the radio stations were just static. Now I knew this was MUCH larger. I went inside and turned on a battery powered radio to the large news channel and started listening...they were having traffic and weather together and just chatting away. A few minutes later they finally announced there was a major black out in the Detroit area and the AP wire was reporting blackouts in other states. Now certain that this was serious, I began to get my emergency communications (Amateur Radio) equipment together because I knew that I'd be needed in the City of Warren Michigan Police Emergency Operations Center (EOC). I am a member of the Civilian Emergency Response Team (CERT), an organization President Bush made nationwide after the 9/11/2001 attacks. Each CERT team is a team of local individuals with training.

Traffic Everywhere.

This is what I find, grid lock. It was rush hour and the majority of the intersections were snarled up, traffic was horrible and moving slow. Luckily, I had already planned, and had ridden my bike many times, on a side-streets-route to the police station. So, avoiding all of the major intersections and arrived at the police station about 20 minutes after I left the house. It was taking people many HOURS to get from one side of the city to the other. In a situation like this, the highways were flowing very well but as soon as anyone tried to get off the highway it was jammed up. The traffic situation lasted for 3 or 4 hours, as soon as everyone got home, no one left and the streets were very easy to travel. Communications systems were also VERY messed up. On 9/11/2001 many of the main phone lines did not work but the cell phones were working. This was because the majority of the NY city had power. 9/11 was a localized event covering square miles in each terrorist event location. This event covered entire states. All of the cell towers and communications centers lost power and those that did work were overwhelmed. In less than a minute after the event started I could not get a hold of the director of our CERT team. The default policy in an event like this is for all CERT personnel to report to the police station with their emergency equipment and gear. On arrival at the EOC less than 30 minutes after the event began the EOC was getting set up and manned. The emergency telephones were being plugged in and the police have a dedicated diesel generator to power the building. We had a TV with other information available and all of the critical city people were coming in.

Since everyone's cell phones did NOT work, we relied on the regular phone lines. However, we had the Amateur Radio Emegency Serivice (ARES) station on the air with the flick of one switch as soon as I arrived and said into the radio, "Net control this is KA8WXR Warren EOC." The HAM ARES net was on the air and our unit at the EOC was ready to go. Why is this important? Historically, the regular phones will only have battery backup from the phone company for 4 to 18 hours. We had to plan on loosing the landlines if this continued on through the day. The HAM radio network would allow us to talk to all of the other EOC's in the area and really, if we had to, to talk anywhere in the world we needed by relaying messages OUT of the affected area.

The Warren EOC. Who shows up at an EOC? The director of emergency services, the mayor and his deputies, the police commissioner, the fire commissioner, directors of staff, public works, water and sewage, communications and all of the other city functors. The police chief and fire chief move in and out depending on what they are doing. An EOC is a central hub of control, logistics and information.

This is how the blackout started for me. Describing the events in the EOC is not all that educational because most people have to deal with the disaster themselves which is what this document is going to describe, what was missing and how we replaced lost abilities or dealt with the power failure and how to deal with what will be worse NEXT TIME.

I should note that I was the only person who had his own personal water and food in my ' ready kit ' in the EOC. Water became an issue FAST and I had my own that I could rely on. We all got hungry later and had food brought in from a deli but I still was the only one with something to snack on in my backpack. There were a few people I ran into who just did not eat for 12-18 hours during the evening and night. The pizza they had the evening of the disaster in the EOC and the pizza they had at lunch time in the EOC was the only food they had to eat, partly because they did not have time to eat. If the EOC was unable to get food due to other circumstances, or if the disaster went for many days, workers would have been hungry. They would of still done their job, improvised and adapted, but it sure was easier to have some food with me under my own control (which I ended up sharing with others anyway.) The people in the EOC were hard working and dedicated and over came all problems.

WATER AND SANITATION.

After the loss of the cell phones individuals started to notice the lack of water pressure. In the Warren area, which is close to Detroit where the pumping stations are, we had very low water pressure. It was flowing about 1/10th the normal rate. This was enough to flush the toilets, it was enough for average citizens to get water to boil for drinking. There was water. Further down the water distribution line (further from the lake) was Novi and other communities. They had NO water. NONE. Turn on the tap and nothing comes out. This means no water to drink, no water to bath with and NO flushing of toilets.

In this country NO ONE should be caught without water to drink in their house. In this day of terrorism and infectious disease and after the HUGE education everyone got about their vulnerabilities to the infrastructure prior to Y2K EVERYONE should have some water. This is so simple that every child would do it if only the idiot adults did not stop them from doing it.

SODA BOTTLES for WATER.
Soda bottles are a miracle of modern material science. There is hardly a plastic better than the formulation used for SODA bottles. These do NOT degrade, DO take hard impacts and can withstand very high pressures. All the average person in a city has to do is take an empty soda bottle, rinse it out well with fresh water from the tap, to remove any sugar or soda, and then fill it with cold tap water, cap it and put it away. NO chemicals, no bleach no anything added. The chlorine in normal city tap water is enough protection. Even most well waters will store JUST FINE without anything being added. The water does NOT need to be changed every 6 months, every year or even every 10 years. If there are NO bacteria or growth medium for the bacterial in the bottle then there will be no water contamination issues. Plain water does NOT go bad. All water is at least as old as the last ice age and individual water molecules can be millions of years old, it does not spoil. Everyone caught thirsty has no excuse for not using empty soda or juice bottles for holding water. Don't use milk cartons for two reasons. 1: they degrade in 6 to 18 months and will leak. 2: Milk can never be fully rinsed out of the carton and it is a good growth medium for bacteria. Start storing some water TODAY. A gallon per day per person is the normal suggestion, more for very hot or cold climates. Generally 1/2 gallon will be drank by a normal adult person and the other half will be needed for food preparation and sanitary reasons.

This photograph is from water at my house. I don't know if YOU want THIS MUCH, but I have a fair amount. Enough to share with people. I DID end up drinking MY water from MY supply during he blackout. It was VERY hot. I came home from the EOC in the middle of the night and was helping neighbors, I was running around a lot so I got quite thirsty. All I did was open a bottle, which was cool from being in the basement, and I had as much water as I wanted.

NOT THE BATHTUB.
Don't be stupid, don't fill the bathtub up with water to drink, maybe for flushing, but not drinking. Most bathtubs are either dirty (according to women) or have chemical residues. Want water fast? Put non-treated-non-scented plain plastic trash bags in boxes, drawers, plastic totes or any container and fill it with fresh water to drink before you loose all of your water pressure. Tie the bag shut. Dip in a glass or bottle for water when needed.

Sanitation Issues

THAT IS NOT ORANGE GATORAID!!

In a no water situation people tend to use the toilet and then cannot flush. The result is a cesspool of fecal material and urine that stinks the house up fast. This is easy to remedy.

First, piss in a bottle. For men, a gator aid bottle or a juice bottle with a WIDE mouth works best. 3 liter soda bottles work ok but require more careful aim. For women, get a large 99 cent funnel in the automotive department at Wal-Mart. This gives the squatting female a much larger target to hit and the urine still goes in the bottle. When done, cap the bottle and put it aside for re-use.

HOW TO MAKE URINE NOT STINK.

A little secret here, urine does NOT contain bacteria. It is STERIL when it leaves the human body. The urine contains nitrates and other minerals that are a growth medium for bacteria. The waste products of the bacteria is what stink. This is true for your underarm when you have body odor as well as when urine starts to stink. Pouring a little hydrogen peroxide or isopropyl (rubbing) alcohol, or bleach or some other antibacterial substance in the bottle will prevent any bacteria from growing and the urine will NOT stink. If it stinks, you did NOT add enough, add some more. I HAVE tested this. I have added iodine treatment from a water treatment product called POLAR PURE ($12 at a REI) and the urine did NOT stink even after 4 months of storage. Yes, I sniffed and tested it, it smells just like 'salt water'. No odor at all.

If people are going to have a hard time pissing in a bottle, then wait a half hour, they'll use it or…. use a bucket. A trash bag in a bucket with some of the antibacterial methods I just described can be used as a 'piss bucket' all day. Just go empty the bucket outside in the evening. Urine can be dumped almost anywhere, on the grass, down a drain etc… Fecal material should be buried.

Number one or Number two? Number two. The harder issue. Many people will be come constipated when there is a lack of bathroom facilities. This is fine, the body is capable of holding this material for days with NO problems in a healthy person but the real answer is to either place a plastic trash bag in the toilet bowl (under the rim of the seat) or place a trash bag in a bucket (3 gallon to 5 gallons) and to place two 2x4's about 12" long across the bucket as a seat. Actually, 2 2x4's about 12 - 18" long over a bucket in a ' V ' shape is very comfortable and most people won't object. Either dispose of the fecal material outside right away or… place a few inches of water in the bottom of the plastic bag in the bucket and use a 1/4 to 1 cup of bleach in the bucket. This will inhibit the bacteria growth and dispose of this at the end of the day. For fecal material (and farts) it's the Hydrogen Sulfide (H2S) that we produce that stinks (rotten egg smell). This dissipates rather quickly and then its bacteria growth that makes the cesspool begin to stink. Control the bacteria, and the stink will be controlled.

I don't know if this is TMI (Too Much Information) I simply want the reader to understand the PRINCIPLE rather than specifics. Better to read it here than to find out the hard way.

The Refrigerator

After people notice their cell phone is not working, the water is not working and the pressure on their bladderis increasing, they begin to notice their belly rumbling and you start hearing, "What about my refrigerator." Forget the refrigerator! It usually has a day or two of food in it and it usually takes that long for it to warm up and then even longer for items to begin to spoil.

Eat out of your refrigerator and freezer first and eat the ice cream first (twist your arm harder right?). Keep the darn door shut unless you need something and don't go spend $500 on a generator for $100 in food in a refrigerator or freezer. A large chest deep freezer full of ' high value meat' will stay frozen for 2, 3, 4 days. Throw some blankets over it to increase its insulation factor. If you do loose food, most of the time your home owners insurance will cover the loss.

The health department put out a notice that stated, "If food as been warmer than 40°F for two hours then throw it away." This is such bull crap that I cannot even begin to comprehend the stupidity. In the middle of a potential power failure where food and water are potentially unavailable for days or a week (See the "You Have No Concept Page") why tell people to throw out the only food they have? This is like telling a person floating on the ocean after their ship sinks that their life jacket may spring a leak in a few hours so they should get rid of it now and tread water manually. My refrigerator is about 42°F most of the time, NOT below 40°F... The ambient temperature of the house was 90-95°F during the day and my house had no power to the refrigerator After 34 HOURS my refrigerator was 63.5°F and my freezer was 53.0°F. I just moved my milk and butter from the refrigerator to the freezer and it was nice and cool, not cold, but cool and I opened both doors about 10 times over those 34 hours. I just started eating my lunch meats, bread and drinking the milk. There is NOTHING wrong with 53°F milk, there are places in the world that WISH they had constant 53°F storage of milk. Most cheese and butter is pasteurized and does NOT spoil fast and eggs can stay just fine for OVER a month in the shell. Once eggs are open and mixed (like in egg salad or mayonnaise) it can spoil, but not in a shell. Just start cooking your meat on the BBQ or gas stove and eat it. If anything becomes stinky or has something growing on it or tastes funny then DON'T EAT it. In a world where we eat 'aged beef ', which is rotted meat, and people order rare steaks it seems STUPID to throw out meat that has been above 40F for two hours. Use common sense. If you have too much meat or ice cream to eat before it melts or really gets spoiled then give it to your neighbors to eat, especially if they'll cook it for you.

Putting food aside to store is VERY easy and the discussion on the subject is a little long. For a FREE, COMPLETE class on putting food away for an emergency, get the MP3 Audio of my last Family Preparedness class (FOR FREE) at **KnowledgePublications.com**

It is fun and easy to listen to and I cover ALL of the subjects needed for protecting your family and loved ones in time of a disaster. Remember, I gave the class BEFORE the black out, listen to what I have to say about milti-state power failures.

The Constant Drone of Generators

Generators are ok for thunderstorms that cause blackouts for a few days, or even a week but power failures that are statewide, multistate or nationwide are a MUCH different story.

When a tornado hits and power is knocked out to 500,000 out of 2.4 million customers then generators can be helpful and many people run these for 24 hours a day. When all 2.4 million customers, and multiple states affecting 50 million people, are out of power then a generator should NOT be run for 24 hours a day.
A refrigerator or freezer does not even need to be run for 1 hour out of 4 to keep everything cool.
Cheap gasoline generators are hogs when it comes to gasoline consumption and will use a great deal of precious gasoline that cannot be replaced. Even with a light load on the generator lots of fuel is used.
Generators should be saved and run only for a few total hours a day when a large TV, the refrigerator and/or freezer needs to be run or food needs to be made (mixer, grinder, blender, microwave, but not an electric stove). Starting the generator and having the neighbors over for a movie party is a great idea. Pop some pop corn, get the food out of the freezer, cook it up and put in a DVD and enjoy yourself. This might be 3 or 4 hours per night.

This is a photograph of a man with a $1000 generator to power his whole house and he owns 5 gallons of gasoline and he does not have any more.

His generator has just become a wheel barrel because he CANNOT GET any MORE GASOLINE. NONE is available. Not in Warren, not in Detroit, not in OHIO and even if it was 100 miles away most people did not have enough gas to drive 100 miles to Lansing and back. (in very slow traffic with no traffic signals).

YOU ARE STUCK.
You cannot leave, you cannot drive OUT of the black out area. The airports are not working. On 9/11 the only way across the country in less than 4 days was to DRIVE. During the Blackout of 2003 there were NO FLIGHTS in the affected states and you COULD NOT drive out of the area due to lack of gas and initial congestion on the highway if you wanted to.

YOU ARE HOME AND STUCK and have a limited amount of gasoline. Don't waste the gas in the generator just to have the comfortable sound of its humming in the background as the kids watch cartoons so you can sit down and feel good. When are you sucking on a hose to get gas out of a car to run your 4 watt monster chasing nightlight all night long you won't feel so safe and comfortable.

After 3 or 4 days when you have no gas, no power, no food, no water and NO LIGHT and your kids look at you, you won't feel so good. Ration your fuel.

The PANIC for Gasoline

This is a line for gasoline on Hoover Road south of the 696 Highway over 1/2 mile long. Any rumor of a gas station with power had people coming from tens of miles away. People ran out of gas while waiting in line. The police had to close stations and roads so fire trucks could use some of the main roads. The arrow points to the gas station.

Fights frequently broke out at gas stations. The worst was when the power was coming back on, a AAA survey found that 9% of the gas stations were open and pumping fuel. Before this 0% of the stations were open but people drove around looking for fuel even though Consumers Energy said that all 2.4 million of its 2.4 million customers had NO electricity. Black marketing was also common. People would fill up a 5 gallon can for $8 in gas and walk across the street and sell it for $20. Special lines formed at pumps for people who ONLY had a gas can. Some of these lines were 300 people long! Any gas station that got power ran out of fuel in an hour or so. Those stuck in the 4 hour line would stay there in hopes of a gas truck coming soon. Some people stayed in line all day and got nothing but an empty tank from idling the car in the 95°F heat with the car A/C on. Imagine if this was NOT a 36 hour black out, with the power starting to come back after 24 hours, but a ONE WEEK black out. The reaction of the public for gasoline was panic, they HAD to have it, even if they did not need it. They had to have it. It was FEAR driven. Please… don't let your generator run 24 hours a day and then go fight for gas to keep the Nintendo and DVDs going for the kids.

This is the definition of a Pedestrian. A person on foot, with no motor transportation. This man is walking and walking looking for gas. He might be a local resident needing gas for a generator or a driver looking for fuel in a now stranded car. He cannot get home. Either way, he's only got a 3 gallon can and that I guarantee you is empty. If you think people fight for gasoline, wait until a longer disaster, a 48 hour one and watch them fight for water. Wait for a 72 hour disaster and watch them fight for food. Wait for a 96 hour disaster and watch them kill for gas, water and food.

Surviving the Blackout of 2003 (c)2003 www.KnowledgePublications.com h2fuel@mail.com

You have NO Concept, None!

For the people who were involved in 9/11/2001, for those who where involved in the Blackout of 2003. For the city officials, the police, the fire and the ordinary people; you have no concept of what a real disaster is.

If you are surprised to hear about people fighting for gasoline, wait until a longer disaster, a 48 hour one and watch them fight for water. Wait for a 72 hour disaster and watch them fight for food. Wait for a 96 hour disaster and watch them kill for gas, water and/or food

As I stated earlier, 9/11 was a disaster in terms of square miles. The 2003 Blackout was millions of square miles and 50 million people. It struck our hearts to watch 9/11 on TV but we were not thirsty or hungry or freezing.

It can't happen? We normally have 1 emerging infection every 40 years. We've had three new emerging infections in the USA in the last 3 years. West Nile Virus, SARS and Monkey Pox. We've had a power outage that was not seen on this scale since the 1970's. Think it can't happen again? It can happen next week only this time it could be 1/2 the country. Who's to say it wasn't computer terrorism bringing down the grid. We proved this could happen. Who's to say it won't be computer terrorism next time.

A 20 person terrorist operation (like the one on 9/11) could bring down multiple points of our power grid at key points across the country all at the same time. Once the grid is tripped, it takes about 18+ hours to start getting it going again. If main lines are damaged, or mined with explosives, snipers or chemical or biological weapons, it could take weeks to repair.

It's not the nuclear weapon that really kills people, it's the loss of the infrastructure that goes down from the blast wave and the fires that kill people. No power means no food, no water, no sanitation, no fuel, no communications, no transportation. This means no health care, rampant infection that always accompanies a disaster (cholera, dysentery, other infection) and without medical care people die. Lets try this exercise in the middle of winter over 1/4 the USA in the northern portions like the 2003 Blackout. Many would die of the cold. No power means no heat.

Imagine a SARS outbreak in the USA this winter so bad that people do NOT want to go to work, to the grocery store, to school, to friends, neighbors or relatives. Try fixing a power grid in the middle of that. Masks are not going to protect you from other people. You better wear goggles as well. The ocular membrane (eye) is a prime route for infection. For a FREE audio class on SARS and protecting yourself, go to **KnowledgePublications.com**

In a speech given by one of the best professionals in the civil defense business at the 2002 Doctors for Disaster Preparedness, Dr. Wood was asked about smallpox by a man and in exasperation over the man not understanding the seriousness of the subject he said, "You're helpless. You don't have a chance, you'll die like slaughter sheep."
A copy of the audio is available at USAHome Land-Defense.com Start your family Preparedness TODAY. You Have NO Concept!

Grocery Store, Money and ATM's

In the audio of my free Family Preparedness Seminar at StevenHarris.net you'll hear me ask the class to open their wallet and purse and tell me how much money they have. While a few people out of 40 had over $100 the average was $10 to $25 per person. When the power went down and the cell phones went down and the water went down so did all of the credit card ability and the ATMs. You can only buy items with the money you have in your wallet. The event started after 4 pm EST on 8/14/2003. At 7 am on the 15th the Kroger's grocery store on Hoover south of 696 got their power back. I took this photo around 1 pm in the afternoon. The Kroger's Corporation and the area manager, Noah King, and their emergency operations team deserve a HUGE gold star for what they did. They packed their shelves and had special deliveries of food and water shipped all evening and night and morning to the store because people were in need AND they knew when the power came back on they'd be swamped. During the black out they only accepted cash and checks. NO credit cards could be accepted. Imagine this going on for 3 days let alone a week. The shelves WOULD be bare, the lines would have been longer, fights would of occurred for food and water just like it DID for gasoline after ONE day. The grocery store was not even without power for 15 hours and look at the line of people. When I was there, bread was very low, so was milk, half the meats were gone (people with BBQ's) and the water shelves were empty BUT... water was coming in by the pallet load and was up front and plainly available. Ever see piranha fish gut a cow to the bones?? That's what people did to the CASES of

water before my eyes. Do you want to be fighting the masses with $20 in your pocket and a car running on fumes or do you want to have a little bit of your own preparation for a disaster.

Surviving the Blackout of 2003 (c)2003 www.KnowledgePublications.com h2fuel@mail.com

There are words that describes these people you see in many of these photos; helpless, desperate, vulnerable and victims. After these words you'll find; causalities, incapacitated and dead.

Despite the role model quality exhibited by the Kroger corporation, this excellence will only benefit the people for so long. When the trucks cannot get in the food cannot make it to the warehouse and from the warehouse to the store and the people themselves cannot get to the store, then there are going to be real problems.

After you listen to the free Family Preparedness class you'll never go hungry again in your life. You'll be able to make the simplest food with the cheapest of materials that store for years and decades. The bread is gone, but you'll have your own bread in as little as 10 seconds. Enough bread for an meal for the entire family for the whole day for less than one dollar. It is worth listening to, or would you rather spend your time listening to the dixie chicks on the way to work.

People lined up at the bank when it finally opened.

People never really got the concept of NO MONEY in many of my classes. It did not hit home until they only had $20 in their pocket and they had to buy 20 gallons of gas at $1.50. Imagine how much gas you'd get if the price was $5.00 a gallon due to prices being raised in a crisis. Some things will not be available at any price and all of the money in the world will not buy the food, water or gas you need. Even if you did have a bunch of money you'd be subject to the theft of it by someone who is hungrier than you are. Desperate people do desperate things. However, now that everything is "back to normal." Food, water, batteries, fuel, stoves, tools and more are at world record inexpensive prices. It's a lot easier to buy the stuff you need now than to pay for it with dollars, your health or your life later.

Imagine going to dial 911 and the phone does not work. The cell phone does not work and maybe if you called 911 the operator may say that they could not get to you for hours. You are on your own. Time to take that Red Cross or American Heart Association First Aid and CPR class. What you have between your ears you cannot loose.

Surviving the Blackout of 2003 (c)2003 www.KnowledgePublications.com h2fuel@mail.com

I Plugged My House Into My Car

This is a true statement. I really did this. I came home about midnight from the Police EOC and I plugged my house into my pickup truck. For those of you who don't know me, I was development engineer in the Scientific Labs of Chrysler / DaimlerChrsyler Corporation. Not only did I work in vehicle development related functions but I worked around and knew the people in electric vehicle and hybrid electric vehicle groups. I now consult professionally in the hydrogen, solar, fuel cell, reformation field as well as other aspects of energy work and other automotive work. I understand energy very well. I travel the USA for a month every year in the summer and I usually go to the West and the desert Southwest. Its HOT there. 117°F during the day, 105° F at night. I like to sleep at 65°F so I have an A/C unit on my little trailer and I power it with a diesel series Hybrid electric generators I made. I came home and plugged my truck into the house and powered it up off the truck and batteries, I did not even start the generator. Not for lack of fuel, it only uses 1 gallon per 7 hours of running a 600 watt A/C unit

Diesel hybrid generator in my vehicle. Its mounted here all the time.

(yes, *I* measured this myself.) If you *REALLY* want details on the generator it is described in detail in my book "Sunshine to Dollars" available at www.KnowledgePublications.com.

My 1997 Dodge Dakota, 1963 Sierra II camper and a 1968 Benson AutoGyro on the back of the truck.

I'm not going to convince you to do the nerdy stuff I do for my research but I am going to show you how to do this with YOUR vehicle for as little as $28 or less. The principle is sound and my neighbors used it to light their house quite well during the blackout. Your car is designed to drive over 100,000 miles and it costs many tens of thousands of dollars brand new. It is made better today than ever in history. It will sit in your driveway and idle just perfectly. It makes a heck of a generator.

The Harris Hybrid Home Generator Made SIMPLE.

In the photo you see a DC to AC "INVERTER". Plugging this into the car power outlet (looks like a cigarette lighter but does not require the key to be on for power) generates 120 volts of modified sine wave "AC " at the 120 volt outlets on the front of the inverter. Plug an extension cord into this and run it into the house. Any cheap cord from the store will work well. My favorite is the bright orange 16 gage, 100 foot extension cord for about $8.00 from Home Depot. Get this through your head, it does NOT have to be a heavy cord, the inverter only produces 300 watts max and only 150 watts through the power outlet plug in the vehicle. If more than 150 watts is needed then the inverter needs to be connected directly to the battery with a pair of alligator clamps, but you don't need more than 20 watts most of the time. See that light bulb in the photo. That is a 7 Watt compact florescent bulb, and I think it is too big. I prefer to use 3 watt chandelier Compact Florescent (CF) bulbs. The 7 watt CF lights a large room up JUST FINE. Its about as bright as the average Coleman lantern and it can be turned on and off on and off at will without relighting it and it is NOT a fire or a carbon monoxide threat. A small car battery is rated about 30 amp hours at worse. Lets say you only want to use half of this before you start the car to recharge the battery. Then two 5 watt bulbs plus the inverter power will be close to 12 watts. 12 watts divided by 12 volts is 1 amp of current draw. We have 15 Ampere Hours (AH) to play with so 1 amp for 15 hours is 15AH. That means you could run 2 bulbs for about 15 hours before starting and idling the car. Idle the car for about 1 hour to replace the energy lost. A truck battery would be closer to 60AH and thus would have about 30 AH to use. If a TV is to be powered (like a 19 inch TV) this could draw around 120 watts. 120 watts / 12 volts is 10 amps. DON'T even THINK of pulling this amount of energy from the battery by itself. You'll fall asleep and drain your car battery and then you'll be YELLING AT ME and I don't want that. If more power than...oh... lets say 15 to 25 watts is going to be used then just let the car idle outside while the TV or the FAN or something larger than 15 watts of lights is being used. This will prevent the vehicle from getting a dead battery.

EVERYTHING THAT WAS USELESS BECOMES USEFUL AGAIN.

This is the real reason for the inverter. All of those personal electronic devices that were useless or did not have batteries are now useful. Power an AM/FM radio, small TV (like a $20 black and white TV), charge your cell phone(if the cell phone system is working), or run your laptop computer. This method is NOT going to power your furnace, microwave, refrigerator, freezer or hair dryer BUT will give you back all of the little things you lost. Playing a jambox with some tunes does not use much energy and can be a big moral booster. During the first week of a disaster people are constantly listening to the news. This inverter can cost from $20 to $50 depending on the store. Walmart, Kmart, BestBuy and other stores all carry the devices. The one in the photo is a 300 watt inverter.

(Above) This is a little 75 watt inverter I got at Gander Mountain for $20 on sale. I've seen it at Bestbuy for $30. I've also gotten 400 Watt inverters at Sams Club for $28.00. I'm using this little 75 watt unit to run a small 5 watt CF lamp in my den.

As a different method, I used a simple 115AH deep cycle marine battery ($55 at Costco, $65 at Autozone) hooked up the 75 watt inverter making 120 volts for the 5 watt CF bulb (in the lamp) and the 12 volts from the battery is charging my cell phone (not pictured but you can see the cord) and it is powering a 120 volt /12 volt / or battery operated black and white TV / AM / FM radio ($25 at Walgreens). It also powers a 1 hour NiMH AA/ AAA battery charger that I used to power smaller HOME radios and lights. I'll describe the selected usefulness of AA's around a house, but AA's are NOT for a ' real ' emergency. I did use this marine battery method during the blackout even when I had my truck powering the house.

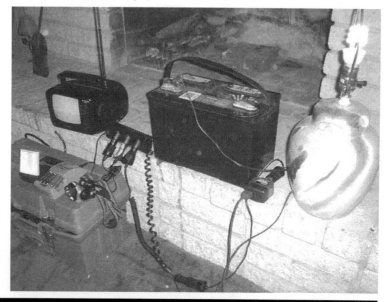

Illumination Around the House (14 Years of Light)

In this book when I talk about flashlights and radios and in my classes I give (free audio version at http://www.KnowledgePublications.com) I'll say that if I find one of these SILLY LITTLE LED lights with AA or AAA batteries in it in your EMERGENCY KIT that I will firmly place my foot in your rear end. If I find rechargeable batteries of ANY type in your EMEGENCY KIT I will do the same thing. ONLY D CELL Alkaline batteries are to be in flashlights and radios for your emergency kit that you will entrust your life with. Sitting around the house and sleeping is not a LOST CHILD emergency or a HELP ME NOW emergency. We all have a great deal of items around the house that use AA or AAA batteries. CD players, color LCD TV's, game boys, small flashlights and even silly little LED lights and head lamps. Listen CAREFLLY. This is for AROUND the HOUSE ONLY when your are 'waiting' for the disaster to calm down. Disasters are like combat and can be 98% boredom and 2% terror. There are MANY AA/AAA NiCD and NiMH battery chargers and the ONLY two I like are the Rayovac 1 HOUR charger (it MUST say 1 hour) and the brand that says DIGITAL on it which is really a MAHA brand charger. The MAHA charges in about 2 hours. Many of the 'others' can take 8 to 16 hours and this is TOO LONG for a disaster home situation. The light on the left is a Rayovac 3in1 headlight that runs for about 100 hours on 1 white LED, 150 hours on 2 red LED's and about 2 hours on the incandescent (brighter) bulb. These times are for the 700mAH NiMH batteries I have in it. Use it for 50 hours and then put the 3 AAA batteries in the charger and the batteries are charged in less than an hour. The charger can be plugged into the car or the marine battery and don't even think of needing to run the vehicle while this charges. It sips power. Get 8 to 16 AA NiMH batteries and use them all you want, all can be recharged FAST and with almost NO effect on your car. I did the math, and remember I'm an automotive and energy professional. If 1 gallon of gasoline was used to idle a car and then to charge the AAA batteries for the Rayovac headlamp and the batteries would last for 100 hours on the single white LED, then after ALL of the HORRIBLE efficiencies of idling the engine, alternator, battery, charging etc...one gallon of gas would give 14 YEARS of illumination (24 hours a day.) Your car, some gasoline and a ONE or TWO hour AA/AAA charger and 8 or more batteries will give the average home a great deal of energy to be used in all of the little things around the house that make a disaster much nicer. The Rayovac 1 Hour charger costs about $30 to $35 and it is at Wal-Mart and at Walgreen's as well as Target. It comes with a plug for 120 volts AC as well as 12 volt DC cord for the car. The "Digital" version is at Wal-Mart for less than $17 and is in the photo department. This may or may not be on clearance but in July I saw them in Wal-Mart's from Michigan to Oregon to California to Arizona, Texas and the back to Michigan on my trip around the USA. I suggest the 1800mAH "Digital" brand batteries from OfficeMax, 4 for $10 or from Walmart or Target. The "Digital" charger is also at OfficeMax but it is $30.00 and comes with 4 batteries. The Rayovac headlamp I described takes AAA batteries but the little white LED fold up light next to it takes 4 AA batteries. This is $8.00 at Walmart and it is an Eveready product. I thought this was the most stupid, worthless light when I saw it, but I bought one of each light, CF bulb, AA, AAA NiMH battery and NiMH charger I saw and I ended up falling in love with this light. I've read by it every night for months and found it to be very adequate for working on a table or reading or making sure I don't trip over something in the dark. Again, AROUND HOME ONLY, not for searching for lost children and NOT to be used in a 'REAL EMEGENCY' emergency kit.

ONLY D CELL ALKALINES. Why?

A "D" cell alkaline battery has about 14,250mAH (mili-Ampere Hours) of capacity when it is fresh. A AA alkaline has about 2400 and a AAA alkaline has about 1100. See that date on the alkaline battery? It means on that date the battery will have between 82% and 84% of its energy from the day it was made. So if the little LED light would run for 100 hours when the battery was fresh, in about 5 years (on the date) the light would run for about 80 to 85 hours. This is ONLY if the battery is stored at ROOM TEMPERATURE. If the battery is in a refrigerator, freezer or in HOT temperatures (your car, Tucson etc…) then it will have LESS energy. it's a MYTH to put a battery in a refrigerator or a freezer. I don't care what you read or were told. I did the test myself and I spoke to the head chemist at Duracell on this issue many years ago when I was doing some battery research. (Also, I LOVE Duracell batteries, if you life has to depend on ONE brand of battery, make it the coppertop.)

Battery 'Self discharge' time is very important and you MUST understand this. The alkaline will have 80+% after 5 years, the NiMH batteries I just suggested for HOME use loose over 1% PER DAY. That means you'll be at 80% in about 15 to 20 DAYS! NiMH batteries are charged and then used, charged and then used and NOT put away charged for an emergency. Understand?! With the advent of our great NiMH technology, don't bother with NiCD batteries. A NiCD AA is about 600-1000mAH, a new AA NiMH battery is 1800-2000mAH. Watch out for D cell NiMH, many times it is only a AA in a D cell shell and is not over 2200mAH in size. 'REAL' D Cell NiMH batteries are 8000 to 10,000mAH and take a special charger, but Rayovac makes one of those too but it can take 2 days to charge 4 10,000mAH NiMH D cells in it.

Illumination and Power at the Harris House

My name is Steven E. Harris and most people who know me think the E. stands for ELECTRIFIED. I'm a professional in the energy business and I understand electricity and safety associated with electricity. I have a way that I energize my house from my power sources during a blackout that are dangerous for a non-electrician type of person to do. So I'm NOT going to tell you how I do it because I don't want some idiot to electrocute him/herself or their children or pet goldfish. So if you want to energize your whole house contact an electrician and have him put in a disconnect box that is up to code. With that said I'll show some of the advantages to having a house that is energized from an inverter or a generator or a hamster running in a cage.

These are the lights in my bathroom. I have six CF 15 watt bulbs in the fixture and each 15 watt bulb puts out the illumination of a 60+ watt incandescent bulb. Since my house was being powered from an inverter and a battery bank I did not want to waste my battery energy. I manually unscrewed 5 of the 6 lights and just had one working. Even this one is too bright for the bathroom when I'm on battery energy but I did not leave it on long. ALL the lights in my house are CF bulbs and I could walk around my house and just flick on the light switches and I'd have light in the room. This made life MUCH easier.

At COSTCO I found a new white LED nightlight and I had to play with it. The lights were 6 for $10. I got some, loved the light and wanted to buy more just in case I had a blackout (before the blackout). The day of the blackout I bought 12 more. When the blackout happened I had 18 LED nightlights. I would plug one or two into each unused outlet in a room. The lights draw 0.15 watt EACH. Not 15 watts, 1/100th of that. 0.15 watts. This gave enough light in each room that I could walk around and not trip over stuff and I could still see everything in the room. The power consumption of all 18 was less than 3 watts. Below you see TWO lights in an outlet, one right side up and one upside down.

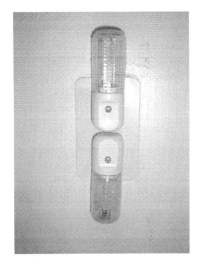

Surviving the Blackout of 2003 (c)2003 www.KnowledgePublications.com h2fuel@mail.com

RADIOS

During a disaster people will be glued to what ever information source available. One of the items I DETEST are the $50 - $100 wind up radios. These promote a false sense of security. The spring life of wind up radios is about 3000 hours. This is about 4 months when used 16 hours a day. Winding one every 30 minutes means winding it over 30 times in one day. I do planning for people and companies who want over a YEAR worth of food, water, fuel and emergency supplies. Having a radio go SPRONG!!! as the spring breaks is just NOT acceptable. The radio on the left is a COBY AM/FM/TV/Weather radio that I got at a discount store for $8.00. It runs on 2 D CELL batteries and will play for over 3 MONTHS, yes, 3 months, 24 hours a day. Yes, I DID the test myself. This is on low volume, not blaring audio. This means that 4 dollars worth of D cells will play this radio for LONGER than the spring life of the wind up radio. This radio uses 2 D cells so 4 D cells will play this radio for about 6 months. This AM/FM/TV/ Weather radio would be worth it if purchased at $30.00. I never used a radio with TV

audio on it during an emergency but we found ourselves listening to it in the EOC all day. Even when we had CNN on the main TV, the communications director would have the radio on the right on the local AM radio station (listening to it on low while on the phone) and the police commissioner liked to listen to a local TV station while he was doing his job and glancing at CNN on the big TV. EOC's are KNOWN for INFORMATION OVERLOAD. The radio on the right is a radio shack AM/FM and short-wave radio. It costs over $50 and I do NOT think this is needed. I had it with me but we never listened to short-wave and since I have a ham radio license and equipment I have better ways of listening. A dear friend and mentor of mine is an AM radio EXPERT. He does what is called Dxing. That is listening for AM radio stations all around the world. He has done this all his life with what we think of as 'old tube type radios.' Back in the old days AM radio was all there was. Not only is he a radio expert but he is an antenna expert. Dave confirms for me that the most simple $8 radio shack AM/FM transistor radio will be able to pickup AM radio stations AROUND THE WORLD if 95% of the other AM stations are off the air (major world disaster.) So the simplest AM radio will always be able to pick up signals from someplace that has power. If I'm in Michigan that means I could listen to California, Texas. Even Australia if the whole USA was out.

COOKING.

I have a whole section on food and cooking in my Family Preparedness Audio Class in MP3 format on my KnowledgePublcations.com website so I won't repeat it here (the class is FREE.). However I will mention that I have a natural gas stove. Since my stove does NOT have a pilot light and there was no electricity, the electric spark ignition device does not work. So I had to light a match and then turn on the gas and light the stove. Don't reverse this order unless you want to loose the hair or skin on your hand. I used my stove for boiling water (in the blue tin cup) and I put boiled some hot dogs and I still had some bread and buns and I snacked on this in between my work at the EOC and helping around home. If you have an apartment or an electric stove or just need a very good, reliable and SAFE source of cooking then I really LOVE a simple $15 to $20 propane burner that goes on a propane bottle. It works just like a gas stove that almost everyone knows how to use. The propane stores forever. The bottle is so safe it is incredible, the burner is cheap and the bottles of propane are cheap as well. $1.50 to $3.00 each (before a disaster!) and will burn on FULL (or high) for about 2 hours. My hot dogs boil in about 3 minutes. This is simple, cheap, safe and will be there when you need it.

NATURAL GAS.

I had a LONG talk with a 30 year expert from Consumers Energy about the natural gas system, at least our system in Michigan. The short story is that the natural gas system is OLDER than the electrical power system. Part of it still has WOOD pipes. Now this sounds funny but the answer is that it is INCREDIBLY reliable. All of the backup systems for the natural gas system are powered by natural gas. We went through EVERY possible disaster all the way up to a mass smallpox plague and 100 million Americans DEAD and no one showing up for work in the control room or doing maintenance. The system will stay up for many months in these scenarios and if the workers can get any where near the system for some basic fixes, it'll stay up for YEARS in a disaster. This means your natural gas oven and stove will work through all but the worst disasters. Listen to the Family Prep class and

why this is important will be fully understood.

Despite knowing this, I still have my propane stove and my other stoves that I have. (yeah.. I have to buy one of every stove so I can tell people which ones are good and which ones are a waste.)

As a fun note, I used the above propane stove for 3 years doing 10,000 miles in one month each year going around the USA. When I travel I eat out of a cooler that I stock from the grocery store and I'm on the back roads SEEING America, not on the highways. So I cook in this burner from one to three times a day and it has never failed me. I even melted the knob and it still works.

MICROCLIMATING
Heating or Cooling JUST YOU in a Disaster

This is a photo of myself Snow Camping. It was 15°F, 30 mph wind and 14 inches of snow falling overnight, and we were warm. In an ideal energy situation we would just heat or cool the air or fabric a few millimeters from our skin. We don't need to cool a whole building or a room, just our bodies. The walls don't care if they are warm or cold.

The same applies in a disaster. We want to heat or cool the person. In the case of the 8/14/2003 blackout and it being SUMMER and 95°F we want to COOL ourselves. During the blackout I would turn on ONE of the dual fans in the window and cool off the bedroom with the cool air from outside, this draws about 45 watts on high. When I went to bed I would use the small fan on the books on low, about 25 watts, to direct air onto me. I would put the window fan on low, about 28 watts and keep the direct fan going. This moved cooler air into the room and then put it onto me. I slept very well. Keep in mind I could of started my diesel hybrid generator and slept in the trailer with the AC (as I do in a 105°F desert at night) but I KNEW that I would be having to TEACH my experiences and adventures to others and I made sure that my experiences would be similar to those of the average person who wanted to be prepared for such a disaster. Have you seen those little hand held fans that run on 2 AA batteries in the store with a little fan about 1 inch in size. A person would be crazy to use expensive AA alkaline batteries in a fan like this during a disaster when the batteries are needed for radios and other devices but since I just showed everyone how to have an unlimited supply of AA batteries with the 1 hour charger, this device is NOW a REAL microclimate tool. Give everyone a $2 personal hand fan to cool themselves and just recharge the batteries. The AA's will run for 4 to 8 hours in one of those little $2.00 hand fans. You can recharge 4 batteries in 1 hour. (the hand fan is not pictured).

MICROCLIMATING
Heating or Cooling JUST YOU in a Disaster

In any disaster, what is the most important item or subject for your preparedness? What is the MOST important thing to have? Most people would say water and they are wrong.

Clothing. Winter weather can kill a person in minutes, lack of water can kill in 3 to 7 days in most cases and lack of food can kill in 2 to 4 weeks. Lack of vitamins can kill in 6 to 18 months. Weather kills in minutes.

As winter weather expert Jim Phillips says, "Clothing is your mobile personal shelter." This blackout was in the summer and it was NOT cold but the next blackout or disaster is not guaranteed to happen only in the summer. The concept of microclimate applies to winter even more than it does to summer cooling. Most people don't have the right clothing to stay in a house that is below 0°F for a long period of time. Sometimes blankets and sleeping bags are not enough. I have done experiments with electric blankets below 0°F in the wintertime, BUT… the blanket MUST be close to the body (maybe just one thin blanket away) and it must have a bunch of blankets or sleeping bags above it for insulation. It is best to have a new, modern, computer controlled blanket that monitors the temperature of the blanket

I actually got a blanket to use less than 60 watts of power (on an average basis) and it got me so warm at 0°F that I had to turn it down even more. 60 watts is the same amount of power the double fan in the window uses. Sleeping bags and electric heating pads on low can be used with an inverter / marine battery or an inverter / car to keep people warm in a disaster.

The other thing that works really nice is to put HOT water into a soda bottle, don't put BOILING water in the bottle. This can burn a person. I use put 130°F water from the tap into a 2 liter bottle and wrap it in a towel for a girl friend of mine who was born in the tropics and had perpetually thin blood. She was always cold in Michigan in the winter. Heating water over a burner, putting it in a bottle and then putting the bottle under the blankets or in the sleeping bag is an excellent way of helping someone keep warm at night, or during the day, in a very cold disaster. Just make sure the water is not too hot and they don't get burned. A burn during a disaster can be deadly. Burns get infected and during a disaster there are lots of extra sources of bacteria and a lack of medical care.

Use the intelligence and common sense God gave you and make your own judgments. Remember, I cannot outline every possible detail in this document.

People who need Electricity to Medically Stay Alive

Some people who are desperately affected by a black out are the people who have home oxygen generators and feeding tubes / systems and those who have a nebulizer for asthma treatments.

It is obvious that most people can go to the hospital and get oxygen or to plug in and get an asthma treatment but there may be a time when the hospitals are overwhelmed or have diseases that you don't want to get within a mile of. In this case there are other places that have backup power. Most fire stations have a backup generator and will accommodate people who need run an oxygen machine or to run a feeding tube or asthma machine. In a disaster the fire department / EMS are pretty busy and it would be best NOT to go there unless it was really necessary. Many large grocery stores have large backup generators and you would be able to find a place to plug in and take a treatment. What is not obvious is that most water plants as well as waste water treatment plants have very very large generators for running the very large pumps it takes to move fresh water or sewage. Many of these are one megawatt in size. The engines are the size of a train locomotive or a small house. They have plenty of spare power to run some medical equipment. Show up and ask if you can plug in, bring your own extension cord and be happy to sit in a chair outside or in your vehicle. Emergency planning personnel for cities should consider these prime places to set up large tents or shelters for taking care of medical patients with needs such as this.

Also, just drive around, many people are running generators and we have all found that disasters bring the best out in people and not the worst. Most people will be happy to allow you to use part of their electricity for a medical purpose. When in doubt, ask. All they can do is say no and who knows. You just might make a new friend. Together we will all come through.

MISC Notes.

Driving at night during a blackout is disorienting. We are so used to seeing stores and signs and lights that we use for land marks it is easy to miss your street. It is a very different experience driving in a major city with no street or building lights. It is not like driving in the country on a dark night. Remember all intersections are 4 way stops.

I have some great ways of making cold and ice with very low power (less than 100 watts) and this can be run from many decent inverters. Most of the parts can be bought for less than $100 brand new or easily gotten for free as scrap. I show this in detail in my book Sunshine to Dollars available at **http://www.KnowledgePublications.com**

The Most Important Thing in Any Disaster.

The most important thing for all of us to have in any disaster is faith. This can be called faith in God, faith in ones self or faith in friends and people who you will never meet.

No matter in what or in who we all must have faith.

Faith that a disaster will bring out the best in people and not the worst.

Faith that solutions will be found to the problems.

Faith that the professionals and leaders will do their job and faith that others will step forth and fill a need.

Faith that we will be able to take care of those who we love and faith that those who we love will come to help those of us who are in need.

Faith that in the darkest moments of despair a glimmer of light will be shown for those in need and that light will grow to be the illumination needed to find the way out of the darkness.

Faith is hard. Especially when buildings collapse and in the span of seconds 3000 people we called mother, father, friend, daughter, son, brother, sister, friend and stranger are taken from us.

When others are taken from us we have even greater responsibilities to the living and we still must do what we can.

I am but one person and I cannot change the world but I will do what one person can do. One person does not have to help at the levels that I personally contribute to civil defense and emergency services but one person needs to do what one person can do when that one person knows he or she has the ability to help.

It might not be during the next disaster or even the one that follows that one. Each person will know what he or she can and should do when the time is right.

Helping during a disaster is not limited to the disaster. The best thing a person can do is to help when an ounce of prevention is worth a pound of cure. The more prepared each person or family is, even if it is just a few gallons of water in each house, is a relief of burden on the people who are coming to help. One gallon of water that you have before a crisis is one gallon that can be given to someone else during a crisis. One gallon of water is enough to keep an infant hydrated for several days. Through disease, dehydration can kill people and children in less than a day.

What makes the difference between whether many people live or die is attitude. I WILL make it, I WILL survive, I WILL help, I WILL be there. It is FAITH that is the backbone for our ATTIDUDE and attitude allows us to make it when things get really tough.

Have faith in yourself, have faith in your friends and family and have faith in those who you will never know.

That which does not kill us makes us stronger.

Together, we will all survive. United we stand, divided we fall.

Five Days After the Power is On: Hey...where is all the food???

I have added this page after I originally wrote the book on August 16th, 2003.

This page is being written on August 20th, 2003. Five days AFTER all power has been restored.

Everything is NOT back to normal. What is missing? Water and food.

Going to the grocery store there are whole sections empty. Whole sections of milk are empty, for some reason all of the 2% milk is gone but the whole and skim is available. Eggs are VERY low in supply and most of the lunch and deli meats are GONE. None available.

Why? Two reasons. 1: Everyone came and bought everything they used up over the 2 days of the blackout. 2: The food warehouses had to THROW OUT many of the meats, milk and other items deemed ' perishable.' Imagine every food warehouse over all of the states affected doing this. When the meats and milk are gone from the store and there are none in the warehouse it takes a week for the trucks to get it from the manufacturing facility and then from there to the warehouses and finally from there to your local grocery store.

Imagine a WEEK LONG blackout. The stores would be empty, the warehouse would be empty, the food manufacturing facility would NOT be operating and the trucks would not have diesel fuel to move the food. Not only do YOU NEED food for the disaster but you need enough food for AFTER the disaster. You might need 3 weeks of FOOD AND WATER under your control for a 1 week long disaster.

Unsafe WATER Means NO FOOD.
For 3 days after the disaster there was a boil alert for all of the water in the Detroit area. Restaurants could NOT serve ANY food that had to be washed. They could not bake with anything that required water in the recipe and they could not server any soda from a fountain because the soda is made from syrup, CO_2 and water.

Any meat or food processing facilities that used water could not process meat or make food.

It comes down to this: During and after a disaster; It is GONE and it is not coming back fast. If you don't have it before a disaster you are not going to have it during and after a disaster.

Are you going to trust those politicians you elected to feed and water your family?

Get over to **KnowledgePublications.com** and get your FREE Family Preparedness Class.

About The Author

Steven E. Harris
Photograph courtesy of May Kearny

Project Destiny
- Solar photons to electrons through hydrogen.
- 95% off the shelf.
- No photovoltaic panels, no fuel cells.
- Made with aluminum, glass, iron, steel, copper, plastic and ceramic.
- 100-year-old technology with 21st Century science, methods and manufacturing.

Steven Harris is a consultant in the energy field. He serves as Director of Operations and Technology for the American Hydrogen Association in the Midwest. After spending 10 years in the Aero-Thermal Dynamics department of the Scientific Labs of Chrysler Corporation, where he was a pioneer member of the group that developed and implemented successful Speed-to-Market development concepts, Mr. Harris left his position to do full time work on the development and implementation of hydrogen, biomass, and solar-related energy systems.

Mr. Harris is currently working with Roy McAlister and others on Project Destiny, a solar hydrogen energy system. He is authoring an upcoming book, "The Positive Promotion of Hydrogen Energy a Model for Success in an Economically Driven Market" and is the author of his latest book, " Sunshine to Dollars." Mr. Harris is the founder and CEO of **KnowledgePublications.com**. In addition to energy, Mr. Harris has a life long commitment to civil defense and the preparedness and protection of the American public. He teaches family preparedness and education regarding threats to the population and lives in Warren Michigan and is available for seminars, teaching and consulting on Family Preparedness and on the subject of Energy.

Mr. Harris's Experience, Projects and a Consulting Portfolio can be found at: **http://www.StevenHarris.Net**

Contact Steven Harris at:
h2fuel@mail.com

Contact Steven Harris at:
h2fuel@mail.com

Or visit:

REAL SOLAR ENERGY

The book that started it all! Free solar panels, energy, heating and cooking at your house. One of the most unique books ever written on Solar Energy. This book will have you building solar heaters in one afternoon. This is the most hands-on book ever written in the field. Get it today. Also includes, at no extra charge, Surviving the Blackout of 2003.

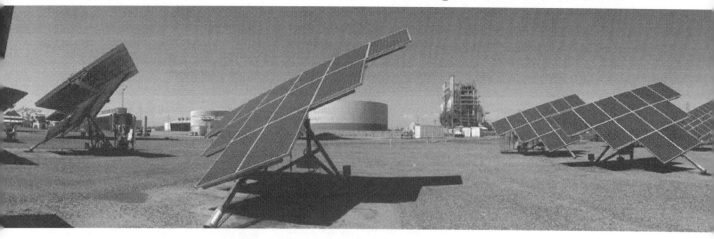

FREE SOLAR PANELS
SOLAR COOKING
SOLAR HEATING

SURVIVING THE BLACKOUT OF 2003 INCLUDED FREE OF CHARGE

KnowledgePublications.com

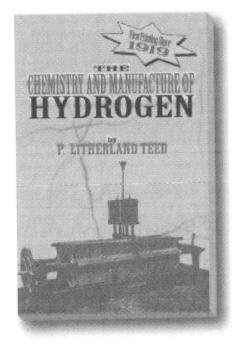

HYDROGEN
FUEL FOR THE LONG ROAD AHEAD

Once again Knowledge Publications has reached into the past to bring to you one of the best books ever written on Hydrogen, it proves that some of the best hydrogen experts ever were contemporaries of your grandfathers and great grandfathers. This is the first printing of The Chemistry and Manufacture of Hydrogen since 1919! With the republication of this book and others like it we are realizing the most fundamental purpose for producing written records: the preservation and rediscovery of knowledge.

KP
KnowledgePublications.com

BOOK AND DVD BOTH AVAILABLE NOW!

KNOWLEDGE PUBLICATIONS
THE WORLDS LARGEST PUBLISHER OF BOOKS ON
HYDROGEN*SOLAR*FUEL CELLS*BIOMASS*ALCOHOL FUEL*WIND

Sunshine To Dollars
Behemoth: The Story of Power
Denatured and Industrial Alcohol
The Mother Earth News Handbook of Homemade Power
How To Save Energy and Cut Costs in Existing Industrial and Commercial Buildings
How to Really Save Money and Energy in Cooling Your Home
Movable Insulation
DOE Chemistry Volumes 1 and 2
DOE Electrical Science Volumes 1-4
DOE Instrumentation and Control Volumes 1 and 2
DOE Material Science Volumes 1 and 2
DOE Mathematics Volumes 1 and 2
DOE Mechanical Science Volumes 1 and 2
DOE Nuclear Physics and Reactor Theory
DOE Classical Physics
DOE Thermodynamics, Heat Transfer and Fluid Flow Volumes 1-3
Effects of Nuclear Weapons
DOE Fuel Cell
Fuel Cells: Power of Tomorrow
Hydraulic Engineering
Hydraulic Motors
Industrial Gases
Industrial Hydrogen
The Complete Handbook of Solar Air Heating Systems
The Solar Cookery Book
Hydrogen Production from Organic Material by Partial Oxidation and Steam Reformation
Mechanical Movements
Hydrogen Generator Gas for Vehicles and Engines: Volumes 1 and 2
Hydrogen Generator Gas for Vehicles and Engines: Volumes 3 and 4
Fabulous Fireball/Experiments With Solar Energy
Construction of Bio-Gas Plants, A Manual
Bio-Gas Volumes 1 and 2
Hydrogen Manufacture by Electrolysis, Thermal Decomposition and Unusual Techniques
Hydrogen Technology for Energy

Fuel Cells for Public Utility and Industrial Power
Hydrogen Generator Gas for Vehicles and Engines: Volume 5
Fuel From Farms: A Guide to Small-Scale Ethanol Production
Energy For Rural Development
The Chemistry and Manufacture of Hydrogen
Biogas Volume 3: A Chinese Biogas Manual
Handbook of Biomass Downdraft Gasifier Engine Systems
Windmills and Wind Motors
Model Petro Engines
Refrigeration and Cold Storage
Philospher Mechanic
Renewable Engines
Solar Heat & Its Practical Aplications
Hydrocarbons from Methanol
Methanol Production and Use
Biomass to Methanol A Specialists' Workshop
HGG Vol 9 Generator Gas The Swedish Experience - Gas 1939-1945
HGG Vol 6 Modern Gas Producer
Applications of Solar Energy for Heating and Cooling of Buildings
HGG Vol 7 Small Scale Gas Producers
The Manufacture of Chemicals by Electrolysis
HGG Vol 10: Ecyclopedia of Biomass Energy
Firewood Crops Vol 1 and 2
Wood Products: Distillates and Extracts
Cellulose: Cellulose Products and Rubber Substitutes
Wood Residue as and Energy Source
Sugars and Their Simple Derivatives
Solar Radiation Data Manual for Flat-Plate and Concentrating Collectors
Microbial Processes
Distillation of Alcohol
Free Alcohol Fuel Compendium Vol 1
BIOGAS Volumes 1-3 CLASSROOM
Chemistry and Manufacture of Hydrogen Classroom Size
Chemical Educator for Chem and Man of H2
Free Alcohol Fuel Compedium Vol 2

COME SEE HOW MANY BOOKS WE HAVE NOW
www.KnowledgePublications.com

USE THE SUN TO HEAT YOUR HOME

Incredibly detailed information on how to make any type of solar air heater. It covers all of the rules of thumb, the materials, where to get them and much more. Whether you're a homeowner or a contractor, this book has everything that you need to know about the construction and operation of all types of solar air heaters for space and domestic water heating. If you're looking for one book that will get you into "hot air," this is the one!

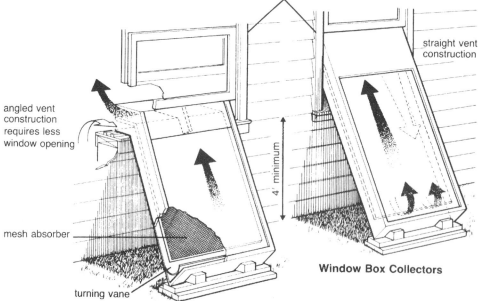

Window Box Collectors

KnowledgePublications.com

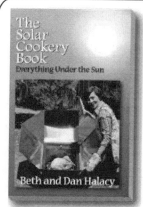

INSTRUCTIONS FOR BUILDING SOLAR OVENS AND RECIPES FOR COOKING IN THEM!

CUT YOUR HEATING BILLS IN HALF

With easy construction plans for easy insulated curtains, a huge variety of panels that you can put inside your windows, outside, and fold up/down and much more. From an extraordinarily talented author, this 379 page book is an absolute must have for any homeowner that wants to stop heat loss now!

KnowledgePublications.com

COOL YOUR HOUSE DURING THE HOT SUMMER MONTHS

Made in the USA
Lexington, KY
30 September 2012